Dedication

This book is dedicated to my son, Richard; not to his memory but rather to the ongoing inspiration that he, and many like him, have given to all those who aspire to serve children.

Richard Hayes: born 12 May 1977; died 7 June 1996. Richard is buried at Katoka Mission Station in south-west Zaire.

Contents

Preface

This book is written so that those students who aspire to be teachers may find their way more confidently through the complexities of the teaching experience. It is based on my own experience of schools over many years, combined with thousands of conversations with serving teachers and education lecturers. I am profoundly grateful to them all.

The book is written for student teachers at all stages of their courses, whether BEd or PGCE, and is designed to be useful as they approach their time in school. It provides an explanation about school life, the demands made on students, the opportunities for them during their school placement, and strategies for gaining success in classroom teaching.

My focus is on primary teaching, but secondary students will, I hope, find much that is of value here. Many aspects of teaching experience are common to both primary and secondary teaching.

CHAPTER 1

The Student Teacher in School

Learning to teach is a very 'public' affair: students' successes and failures are visible to a great many different people – teachers, tutors and pupils

(Furlong and Maynard, 1995)

School experience takes a number of forms, depending upon its stage in the training course and the expectations of college and school. Teaching experience can take many forms, including:

- The structured observation of a child or a teacher at work.
- Working alongside experienced teachers and modelling classroom practice on them.
- A short block of time in school with some responsibility for teaching a specific subject or subjects at designated times in the week.
- A longer period of time in school with responsibilities for most or all of the curriculum.

(Note that throughout this book, the term *curriculum* normally refers to the formally taught curriculum based on the National Curriculum for England and Wales. The term *extra-curricular* denotes activities within school that are outside the formally prescribed programmes of learning.)

This book offers practical suggestions about how you might go about making the best use of your time in your placement school. The majority of it is concerned with aspects of **Formally Assessed School Experience** (FASE), including strategies for developing a professional approach to the job of a teacher through relationships with pupils, colleagues and parents.

REQUIREMENTS

There are specific requirements demanded of all student teachers if they are to gain qualified status and be given responsibility for a class of children. Some of the requirements relate to formal academic study in college (university faculties, institutions of higher education, and so on); some of them to teaching abilities. However, if you are unable to demonstrate your competence in the classroom, college studies will have been largely wasted. Partnership in training involves you, the college and the school (see Figure 1.1). Monitoring and assessment of your progress takes two broad forms:

Formative assessment

On-going assessment in which a supervisor observes you at work in the classroom, provides you with feedback about your teaching, and discusses strategies for improvement.

Summative assessment

A concluding assessment at the end of a series of lessons or a full school experience in which evidence drawn from your ability to cope satisfactorily with the demands of classroom life is evaluated by a supervisor.

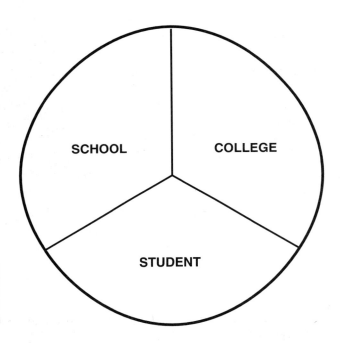

Figure 1.1 Partnership in training

Both assessment types are important. As a trainee teacher, you need support through formative assessment as you attempt to negotiate the twists and turns of classroom and school life. Most teachers are very willing to provide advice, offer comment, point out areas for improvement and give direction for the future.

It can come as quite a shock to a new student to realise how complex the job of teaching is. Far from merely standing up and doing it, the art of teaching requires careful study, consideration of learning theories and the modelling of good classroom practice.

During a FASE, there has to be a summative assessment made at the end of your time in school about whether you have achieved a satisfactory standard in your teaching and professional relationship with other staff. The supervising mentor's summative assessment consists of a written report about the extent to which you have succeeded in relating to the children, organised your teaching, carried out your lessons, taken advice from experienced practitioners, and shown a keenness for the job. The report will highlight your teaching strengths, identify areas for development and note your potential. As such, the mentor's summative comments should not contain any surprises for you, as the on-going discussion should result in agreement about the main points.

If the assessment is necessary for granting qualified teacher status, you must demonstrate your competence in a wide range of professional skills. Your school placements are intended to give you the opportunity to master in a systematic and sustained manner the competences that you require for teaching. Some areas of competence, such as the need to develop and maintain a good relationship with the children, will be evident from the moment you enter school. Other competences, such as assessing children's progress and devising individual work programmes, become increasingly important as you gain further teaching experience. It is impossible to master every aspect of teaching straight away; neither the teachers in school nor your college tutors will expect you to do so.

NOTE: Sometimes the supervisor is a college tutor; increasingly, the supervision is shared between college and school, with a trained teacher from school (the mentor, also known as associate tutor or link tutor) and the class teacher providing regular feedback to you about your progress, with the college tutor acting in a supporting role.

First time in school

Perhaps this is your first formally assessed school experience. You may feel very tentative or you may be keen to get started and show what you are capable of. During your first time in school, it is common for you to concentrate on teaching a narrow range of the curriculum or assisting a group of children with their work. You may be asked by the college to pay special attention to specific teaching episodes, such as the way you begin and end a lesson, the clarity of your instructions, the type of questions you use, and the way in which children engage with the activities you have devised for them. Through careful lesson planning and thoughtful reflection upon your teaching, you will become more aware of the extent of your own subject knowledge, the way you apply it to your teaching, and the strategies to ensure that children learn effectively. As you explore the many dimensions of teaching, you will discover that there is a lot to learn about managing groups of children and ensuring that they achieve high standards.

During your first teaching experience, it is expected that you will establish a good working relationship with the children by talking to them and listening carefully to their responses, questions and comments. You may be asked to plan lessons in certain curriculum areas (often in Maths, Science, English), stimulate the children's interest in the subject area you are teaching, and gradually gain their confidence and respect.

Colleges adopt different approaches: some will use the first experience to eliminate weak or unmotivated students; others pair students and encourage *peer evaluation*, where one student observes another teaching and offers feedback. To avoid misunderstandings, it is important for you to ensure that you know and understand exactly what is expected of you. In every school experience, you will have to evaluate your own teaching (or sometimes that of another student if you are working in pairs) and reflect systematically upon your mistakes and successes.

> **REMEMBER: No school is obliged to accept students. Those who do will normally receive payment from the college, but view the opportunity to contribute to the future of the profession as an important and worthwhile exercise.**

It is common for students on their initial FASE to begin slowly and build up to greater responsibilities. For instance, in your first week, you may be expected to teach only one lesson to different groups in turn or take a single session each day. You may be asked to read a story to the whole class or take them all for a PE lesson. By the *end* of your school placement the expectations will have risen, and you may be required to take responsibility for the whole class over short periods of time, hear readers regularly, work with less able children or supervise a group using computers. Whatever pattern of school experience is specified by the college, it is essential that through it you extend your own learning and understanding of the teaching process.

The first time in school as a trainee teacher can be quite daunting. You should accept every offer of help from the mentor, class teacher and other school staff.

LEARNING FROM EXPERIENCE

If this is not your first FASE, then you have a bank of experience to draw on. Cast your mind back to your first FASE: the tenseness of your meeting with the class teacher; the struggle to convince yourself and the class that you were a real teacher and should be treated as such; the fear of being unable to cope; the pleasing discovery that you could. Not forgetting, of course, those visits from your mentor.

You considered yourself fortunate on that occasion. The school was a relaxed place and the class teacher very supportive. Your mentor seemed to know what she was talking about and gave you sound advice. The trouble was that every time she came to watch you teach, you felt a nervous panic. The lesson that you had so faithfully prepared never really took off; you heard yourself speaking in a strangely unfamiliar tone; your anxiety to get the children down to work meant that you curtailed the important introduction and this led to lots of similar questions from different children during the lesson. As you moved around the room trying to be natural and firm but friendly, you noticed the mentor writing something down on her pad. This only served to increase your tension. Never did the bell take so long in coming!

At the time, those notes were important to you, and you read and re-read them. One or two things that she wrote caused a pang of worry to shoot through and you longed to ask her to explain exactly what she meant, but you were concerned in case she misunderstood your concern and interpreted it as weakness or fussiness. After the time in school had come to an end, your anxieties seemed trivial; but at the time they were a source of concern.

The notes are an important part of your development as a teacher. They may include some encouraging comments that acknowledge your thorough preparation and hard work in maintaining a positive atmosphere despite the potentially disruptive children who used up so much of your time and energy. There may be suggestions about making the lessons more relevant and interesting for the children, using resources more effectively and allowing time for children to explore some of their own ideas. The advice makes more sense in hindsight and gave an opportunity to reflect upon your experience:

- **Why are you doing this activity with the children in the first place?**
- **Have you spent enough time explaining the purpose to the children?**
- **How much are they learning from the experience?**
- **How do you know?**
- **Where next?**

You smile as you recall the nerve-tingling intensity of those early days in school. When the children asked you who you were you did not know quite what to answer, but managed to reply that you were a teacher, a student teacher. The older children smiled knowingly or whispered to their companions: it's only a student! You wondered if you would ever manage; but you did, and now face further time in school, determined to make a success of it. School placements are meant to be cumulative in the sense that they gradually offer you a range of experiences which will result in you gaining sufficient competence to be eventually trusted with a class of your own. So if there are elements from these earlier experiences that are weak or missing, you will need to pay special attention to them in subsequent teaching opportunities. For instance, if this is your second or third teaching experience, new expectations might well include:

1) Planning a **series of lessons** rather than a number of single ones.
2) Keeping some **systematic records** to show the progress of a group of children.
3) Taking responsibility for the **whole class** for an increasing amount of time.
4) Allocating tasks to **other adult helpers**.

Though some of these responsibilities may have their roots in your first school placement, all experiences are a preparation for the time when you will be expected to move from being *a* teacher in the classroom to being *the* teacher. During the final FASE of your course you need to spend extended periods of time (perhaps a number of separate half-days during the early weeks, increasing to every day during the final week) in complete charge of the class. Ideally, your duties should include taking the register, assisting with playground duty, allocating tasks to classroom assistants, keeping records of children's progress and (where possible) reporting to parents about their children's progress and attainment.

Doing your best

Some early teaching experiences are ungraded, in which case you can enjoy the experience far more, knowing that mistakes will not herald the end of your career aspirations but are an opportunity to learn more about the job. If you *are* being assessed and need to successfully pass your school experience, be assured that everyone is keen for you to do well and will give you every opportunity to show what you can do and (just as important) what you are prepared to learn. No-one expects a student teacher to be perfect; such a species of student has yet to be discovered. However, school mentors will want to see you make every effort to work hard and do your best to be the enthusiastic student of their dreams. College tutors and mentors want to ensure that you are willing to persevere, respond to their expectations, and demonstrate that in time you will prove to be worth the considerable investment of time and energy that your training inevitably requires.

As you lie in bed trying to ignore your alarm clock and thinking of what lies ahead during the coming day, it is tempting to convince yourself that you won't be able cope with the range of demands that you will meet in school over the next eight hours. If you ever feel this way, it may be some reassurance to know that it is something shared with many teachers, both experienced and novice. The task of coping with thirty lively young people, each from a different background and with a variety of abilities and expectations, is a challenge for anyone. However, it pays to remember that others have coped, and so will you if you are prepared to learn fast and respond positively to advice. Teaching is a job in which you can never say that you have arrived – there is always the unexpected, the extra step, the search for something better.

Whatever you are able to accomplish during your time in school, it is appreciated by every type of supervisor that some students will progress more quickly than others, and that there are bound to be ups and downs. It is your overall progress and willingness to learn that is at the heart of a good teaching experience. Naturally you want to do your best, but most students are not in the running for a teaching Oscar! It is easy to use up valuable energy worrying or striving for the unattainable when your energy could be better used in gradually enhancing the scope and ingenuity of your lessons over the time you are in school.

Becoming self-critical

Most colleges have developed procedures to enable students, tutors, mentors and teachers in school to work together to provide a much clearer picture of a student's abilities, with a view to helping them remedy weaker areas and build up the stronger ones. To do this, colleges now draw more directly on the students' perceptions of their own progress as well as those of the school mentor. Over the years, teacher trainers have come to realise that the more fully students become engaged with their learning, the more effective it is likely to be. A combination of a supervisor's assessment and the student's own self-assessment is seen to provide a more comprehensive and accurate view of progress than a single perspective. A simple checklist is helpful:

- **How am I doing?**
- **How can I do better?**
- **How can I identify my strengths and weaknesses?**
- **How can I improve them?**

Teachers have one thing in common: they have had to learn many things through making mistakes. By observing experienced teachers, noting the forms of interaction between children and adults, and then carefully reflecting upon the implications for your own teaching, you can avoid some difficulties. This is not to say that you will be able to learn the craft and profession of teaching by passive contemplation. No-one becomes a good teacher just by reading a book like this one! Everyone has to test theoretical propositions about effective teaching in the light of time spent at the chalkface. This process will be enriched if you can use teaching experiences as a stimulus for action rather than for despair. Nothing is gained by brooding darkly over your mistakes.

The constructive use of a **diary** noting key episodes associated with classroom practice is a helpful strategy for improving your teaching. Episodes can be categorised in one of three ways:

1) those directly related to the skills of teaching and learning;
2) those associated with classroom order;
3) those involving relations with adult colleagues.

As a positive means of analysing your experiences, use the following headings:

- A *description* of the episode
- The *causes* and *consequences* of the episode
- The *lessons to be learned* from what happened

Reflecting upon critical incidents is a way of improving your teaching. Classrooms are complex places. There is always a lot going on at the same time and teachers need to be on their toes to keep pace with it all. As you learn to be constructively critical, select common occurrences for analysis using the framework above and use the information to inform future lesson planning and implementation.

It is unhelpful to wallow in the misery of disappointment or glory in occasional successes. Thus, instead of allowing an error of judgement to throw you off course from achieving what you believe to be worthwhile in teaching, use it as a spur to make improvements. Similarly, ask yourself what made your great lesson so good and extract the key elements to use as a basis for future sessions. Perhaps it was the thoroughness of preparation, the appropriateness of the content or the imaginative way you presented the material. Recognise that you cannot expect to get everything right first time. View your school experience as an opportunity that, with perseverance, will transform the good into strong and the weak into better.

Even the most ordinary classroom events provide information about the teacher's priorities, the children's attitudes, the way that learning takes place and the effect upon the classroom environment. Perhaps the organisation is poor, or the children need more encouraging to look after things, or the rules about movement around the classroom need refining, or the classroom assistant is under-used. It is often easier to analyse someone else's teaching than your own; this is why many colleges ask students to observe one another and thereby generate issues for discussion and action.

WHAT IS HAPPENING?
WHY IS IT HAPPENING?
WHAT DOES THIS TELL ME ABOUT LEARNING?
WHAT DOES THIS TELL ME ABOUT TEACHING?

Experienced teachers take many things they do for granted. However, you must cultivate the habit of questioning classroom practices and analysing events in such a way that you will clarify your thinking and be in a position to justify your actions. In addition to knowing about *how* things are done, it is essential to cultivate the habit of asking *why*.

PROFILES

If you are a Postgraduate student (PGCE) you will spend a larger proportion of your time on school placement than undergraduates, and have to build up your expertise more quickly. You need to make the fullest use of your opportunities in each school and gain experience of practical teaching, get advice from curriculum leaders and enter into the wider aspects of school life through attending staff meetings, parent consultations and extra-curricular activities.

If you are an undergraduate you will experience at least 4 different placements and can afford to build your profile gradually, though achieving the same final competence as PGCE students.

During your course of training, you will gradually build up a profile of your own teaching abilities in respect of your knowledge of the whole curriculum, subject knowledge, teaching methods, control and discipline, assessment of children's progress, and relationship with staff and parents (see Figure 1.2). Profiling is a method of recording your present achievements systematically, pinpointing areas for enhancement, and shaping your preparation for teaching. During school placements you will gain a variety of experiences across the curriculum with different groups and whole classes within your selected age phase. You can identify aspects of your teaching which need priority attention by looking back to previous experiences, using advice from teachers and tutors, and comments contained in reports on your work. Sometimes, by your second or third FASE, you may still not have had opportunity to teach certain subjects (Music is a common example), be responsible for the whole class or carry out essential assessment and record-keeping. Or you may have struggled with aspects of lesson planning, classroom

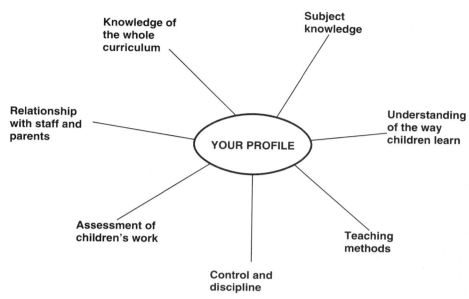

Figure 1.2 The teaching profile

management, lesson continuity, maintaining order, motivating pupils or matching task to ability. Perhaps you will have found teamwork difficult, failed to relate to other teachers or floundered with time management. Profiling helps to identify areas for improvement as well as highlighting strengths.

At the end of your course, you will complete a **Career Entry Profile (CEP)** in which your competence as a teacher is listed under different headings:

- **subject knowledge;**
- **understanding of the way children learn;**
- **planning and preparation;**
- **teaching approaches;**
- **assessment of recording of children's progress**

and wider aspects of your professional role:

- **relationships with parents and colleagues;**
- **knowledge of the Code of Practice for Special Educational Needs;**
- **awareness of your contractual obligations as a teacher.**

The CEP is taken into your first teaching post to provide the basis for your future career development.

LEARNING YOUR LESSONS

If you have already completed a FASE, you will know the importance of properly preparing your lessons (see Chapter 5). However, preparing a lesson plan is of little use unless you are sensitive to a number of factors:

- **The knowledge and understanding the children already possess**
- **The patterns of learning with which the class are familiar**
- **The need to spend time introducing the lesson carefully, checking that you have clarified your expectations and providing work appropriate to the children's ability and understanding**
- **The flexibility to go in a different direction if your plan isn't working**

You won't need any reminding of the challenge that certain children can bring, even to the most dedicated teacher. During previous experiences you will also have appreciated the role played by the class teacher, and worked as a member of a team of teachers. You will have discovered that success during school placement relies on good relationships.

- **It is essential to maintain an open dialogue with the class teacher and mentor, including requests for advice, opinions on lessons and help with children with difficulties.**
- **Class teachers are ultimately responsible for their pupils and will expect you to do your very best to ensure that they benefit from your teaching.**
- **There are other adults in school who play an important part in the teaching and learning process, such as parent helpers and classroom assistants.**

It is easy to become isolated in teaching. Some students meet difficulties or have concerns about how well they are doing, and bottle this up instead of seeking help early on. Your relationship with teachers and mentors will be healthier if you see them as more experienced fellow travellers than as critics.

Whichever stage of your training you have reached, you will enhance your experience by working collaboratively with other students. Mutual support comes through sharing ideas, encouraging one another and giving advice. If you are the only student in the school, or a mature student who has little direct contact with others out of school time, it is worth establishing a telephone link with several confidantes as a means of enlarging your network of friends and supporters.

It may be that a previous school experience went well, or not. Either way, it is important to learn from the past as you approach your next placement. If you struggled last time, don't blame it on the class or the school or the teacher or the supervisor or on yourself. In fact, don't blame anyone. Instead, reflect upon the areas in which you made progress and those in which you struggled. Teaching is a job where we are all learning all the time, no matter how old or experienced we may be. So take a step back and take an honest look at last time.

Q: Did you prepare thoroughly?

If not, was it because you did not know how to go about it, or because you were unwilling? Preparation is not only about having a good idea for a lesson, but also about pitching the lesson at the right level for the children, thinking about your introduction, development and ending, and anticipating the way in which the lesson is likely to unfold.

Q: Did you spend enough time thinking through the organisation of the teaching and learning process

If not, was this due to inexperience, or the special nature of the class situation? Or unexpected factors, or too much responsibility too early? Organisation is not only about setting up a lesson, but also about the detail of how you will manage it, from getting your resources ready before you start to clearing up at the end.

Q: Did you struggle with control?

If so, was it because you treated the children too harshly (and thereby frightened or antagonised them) or too softly (so that you failed to gain their respect) or because the lessons were inappropriate? Teachers use many different control strategies, with varying degrees of success; however, an essential ingredient is maintaining children's interest in the task. This simple truth is, however, easier said than accomplished. Motivating children depends as much on your own enthusiasm and commitment as it does on theirs.

Q: Did you spend more time worrying about imagined problems than working to solve actual ones?

If so, what strategies will you use to maintain a more positive approach next time? The best way to increase your confidence is through classroom success. If you find yourself losing sleep and fretting over aspects of your teaching, write out a list of your concerns and a parallel list of **appropriate action**. Listing concerns without compiling strategies to deal with them will merely increase your stress level.

THE CLASS TEACHER'S AND MENTOR'S EXPECTATIONS

Whatever stage of your course you have reached, it is essential that you clarify the expectations of teachers and mentors in advance of starting your teaching. This is particularly important if you have to relate to several different teachers, as they may have differing views about your role. At the start of the practice, it pays to spend some time clarifying your responsibilities over the weeks, including what you should be doing when you are not actively engaged with the children. For instance, are you allowed to go into the staffroom and write up notes? Are you to act as a classroom assistant? Are there opportunities to sit and observe the class teacher at work or closely assess children's work? Of course, it is also part of a teacher's role to define your responsibilities too.

Misunderstanding between the mentor, class teacher and student over responsibilities is one of the commonest problems during a school placement, despite the tighter agreements now existing between schools and colleges. For instance, you may feel proud that you are spending time in the staff room marking children's work after a lesson instead of sitting reading the newspaper, but if the class teacher wants you to put up a display in the corridor, your good intentions will backfire. The teacher might be saying to herself: 'I can't sit in the staff room after the lesson marking books, so why should that student?'

The same principle applies to many other actions which you may feel are reasonable but might rankle with a teacher. For example, during occasions when you are not responsible for a group of children, even innocent actions can appear to be a dereliction of duty:

- **Going out of school to the local shop to buy a pasty for lunch.**
- **Sitting and looking at the vacancies column in an education newspaper.**
- **Chatting in a corridor with another student or classroom assistant.**

To avoid unnecessary problems, follow the simple principle of maintaining good communication with the teaching staff and taking great care over the impression you create as a trainee teacher. Although your active teaching commitment will increase across the time you spend in school, it is helpful from the beginning to consider yourself as a *full-time* teacher with *part-time responsibility* for lesson preparation and learning. It is unreasonable for a class teacher to ask you to teach without warning, but it is reasonable for you to give some general assistance during your non-contact times. Areas of school life that are not covered by college documentation must be negotiated and discussed with teachers and supervisors throughout your time in school. Aim to show the teachers in the school that you are determined to succeed, while giving them your full support.

THOUGHTLESS BEHAVIOUR

We have seen that developing a strong relationship with other adults in school is an important professional responsibility. Because teaching can be a highly pressurised job, and people are sometimes sensitive to the words and actions of others, it is possible for student teachers to offend or annoy due to thoughtless behaviour.

The initial impression that you create with your host school is vital, and nothing should be said or done which might jeopardise it. Most teachers are very sensitive to criticism and do not take kindly to students whom they perceive as having a negative attitude. The following are examples of thoughtless and negative behaviour:

Critical comments about your initial impressions of a school situation that insult the teachers who have to work there every day

FOR INSTANCE: Your casual comment that the school's swimming pool is small may be true, but fails to take into account the huge effort that staff and parents have made in raising money for building and maintaining it.

Over-zealous questioning of teachers about their reasons for adopting a particular teaching approach

FOR INSTANCE: You may be very keen to use computers in the classroom, but direct questions to a teacher about the reasons for their absence (thereby implying criticism) may overlook the fact that classes alternate half-termly in using them. It is better to ask whether you will be expected to use computers during your teaching practice and comment constructively after the teacher has explained the situation.

Unsmiling passivity that may be interpreted as a lack of interest on your part

FOR INSTANCE: You may be trying to impress the teacher with your cool professionalism, but your blank expression may give the impression that you are bored.

It is important to realise that teachers and mentors do not have time to waste in dealing with uncooperative, lazy or supercilious students. On the other hand, all agree that good, hard-working students who are willing to persevere and treat their responsibilities seriously are worth their weight in gold. Teachers are professionals doing an important job. They deserve respect and a positive response from people who are their guests. Make sure that you create the right impression.

GOLDEN RULE: Impressions count for more than words

Once you begin teaching, it is easy to lapse into thoughtless behaviour that irritates the school staff. The following instances are genuine examples:

1) The student who regularly parked his car in the head teacher's allotted place.
2) The student who kept leaving his empty tea mugs in the classroom.
3) The student who used up the teacher's supply of black sugar paper for mounting pictures.
4) The group of students who descended upon the staff's tea and coffee supplies without asking and expressed surprised when they were asked to contribute towards the cost.
5) The student who never went into the staffroom because she felt embarrassed about talking to teachers.
6) The students who seemed to think that because they were a mature student, they could ignore their mentor's advice.
7) The student who arrived just before the bell each morning and was always one of the first to leave at night.
8) The student who sat in the corner of the classroom painting her nails when she was supposed to be observing the teacher at work.

As unlikely as some of these examples may seem, they are all true. It is surprisingly easy to break the unwritten laws of school life by failing to take notice of the way things are done, giving a poor impression. Most students who get caught out in this way are not acting wilfully, but have given insufficient thought to the consequences of their actions. Take note!

BREAKDOWN IN COMMUNICATION

Very occasionally, your relationship with the mentor or class teacher becomes strained or there is a breakdown in communication with them. If the situation involves the *class teacher*, it is sensible to ask the mentor for confidential advice. When you discuss the matter, do not criticise the class teacher but do be honest about your feelings. The issue is normally sorted out quite easily following the discussion. If you are uneasy about your relationship with the *mentor* or what is expected of you in school, the college tutor is the person to contact. Most circumstances can be resolved by using common sense and courtesy, but if you feel that you are floundering or you cannot see any prospect of improvement, seek help quickly.

THE JOY OF TEACHING

When your teaching is going well, it is like making the winning shot at Wimbledon or scoring the deciding goal at Wembley. Despite all the struggles involved in preparation, then in engaging with the children, the thrill and satisfaction of success is worth the effort.

SERIOUS TEACHING IS NOT THE SAME AS JOYLESS TEACHING.

The most contented teachers learn to balance the seriousness of learning with the joys of building a close bond between themselves and their pupils. Opportunities for celebration should not be missed, not only when children complete work of high quality, but with events such as birthdays, achievements gained outside school and special occasions. You will discover that learning becomes more pleasurable, and children and young people more motivated, if you pay attention to the things that delight and charm their minds.

CHAPTER 2

Teachers, Mentors and Students

The more they identify with their jobs, the greater the satisfaction they receive

(Nias, 1989)

Schools do not operate by magic. There are established routines, procedures and statutory legislation governing what does and does not happen within a school. For instance, the National Curriculum and associated testing applies to all children of school age in maintained schools. Parents have the right to ask for certain forms of information about how the school functions and about their children's progress. School governors, have the power to establish policies for pay, promotion and standards of adult behaviour in school.

RESPONSIBILITIES

Teachers in every school are contractually committed. The resulting obligations mean that teachers are not free agents, and have to work within certain constraints. In addition, there are whole school policies agreed by staff or sanctioned by the head teacher that influence the ways in which teachers act and think. As a visitor, you may not be fully aware of the diverse demands and expectations placed upon the teachers with whom you will work, or the intense discussions which precede agreed decisions. It is important for you to realise that some aspects of school life are fixed, leaving little room for change by individual teachers. Teachers often complain about the excessive paperwork and numbers of meetings in school. Perhaps they have a point. However, they have to balance the competing demands upon their time, and make the best of the boring bits.

When you are a qualified teacher you will face similar dilemmas. For instance, filling in large numbers of report cards may seem to be a waste of effort to you, but as it is a requirement teachers have little choice but to do it. During your time in school as a trainee teacher, bear in mind the heavy commitments that your host teachers have to meet and take note of the coping mechanisms they use. Make sure that you share the burden by working conscientiously rather than adding to it through slackness or unhelpful attitudes.

TEAM WORK

On every school staff, teachers brings their own expertise, enthusiasm and knowledge to enrich the learning environment. You, too, have your own personal gifts, strengths and attributes to offer, and as class teachers and mentors become aware of them, they will draw upon them for themselves and the children. Good teachers are always ready to extend their own understanding and teaching skills by distilling other people's ideas and adapting them for their own use. They are usually delighted if you can offer some teaching expertise that they lack (such as Music, PE or IT) or are willing to attempt something that they dislike teaching (such as swimming and outdoor games) or simply employ some interesting and creative teaching approaches that they had not considered before. In the same way, you will learn a lot from teachers as they demonstrate their skills and employ their tried-and-tested strategies. Teaching must be one of the few professions in which qualified people will freely admit that they have things to learn from trainees. No teacher, however experienced, is too clever or mature to learn from others.

BORN OR CONSTRUCTED?

Few people become teachers by accident. A few drift into it because they cannot think of anything else to do and end up enjoying the job immensely. Others have longed to be a teacher since they were quite young and feel frustrated that they cannot teach without completing a long training course. There are others who think that they want to teach but are unsure about whether it is right for them and need the experience of a school placement to confirm or reject their choice of vocation.

As you contemplate your teaching experience, it is worth remembering that few teachers are naturals; most have to persevere to make the best of their weaker characteristics while building upon the stronger. Some experienced teachers say that they can spot a good student teacher straight away; equally, they claim that they can recognise someone who will never make the grade. All class teachers and mentors, however, are agreed about desirable characteristics in student teachers:

- **bright and keen, confident without being arrogant, and generally enthusiastic about life: teachers are always willing to help students who try hard;**
- **well informed about their subject matter, understanding the intellectual and emotional needs of children: teachers value qualities of organisation, time management and conscientiousness;**
- **can relate well to other adults, including parents and staff: teachers in the twenty-first century must be trustworthy team members, capable of planning ahead and contributing to a group effort;**
- **willing to think for themselves and able to take advice and implement it in a thoughtful and perceptive manner: the most successful teachers can reflect upon**

their mistakes and successes and develop suitably effective strategies as a result;

- **neither too aggressive nor too timid**: some of the best teachers are quiet by nature and do not gain control by loud demands or hectoring, but rather by providing appropriately interesting lessons and understanding the varied needs of pupils in the class. A purposeful, determined student is welcome in every school;

- **can cope patiently but firmly with the demands of individual children**: such students are always commended by teachers;

- **knowing when to use different teaching methods and when to terminate an uninspiring lesson**, or when to be strict and when to accept light-hearted banter with a smile: these qualities normally only come after a lot of experience in teaching.

Students with the potential to be good teachers develop an instinct for teaching and learning that draws upon their life experiences and training. In fact, born teachers are always characterised by their determination to go on learning and improving.

DEMANDS OF THE JOB

Teaching is a tiring and emotionally draining job. There never seems enough time to fit everything in, and considerable effort is expended in maintaining standards, liaising with colleagues, carrying out regular duties, attending meetings, preparing documentation and reporting to parents. For students, there is the pressure associated with lesson preparation, the hunt for resources (such as books), seeking help from tutors, evaluating progress and keeping pace with various writing tasks. There is also the underlying uncertainty about how well they are progressing and whether they are emulating the success of their fellow student in the adjacent classroom. Fear of failure is an ever-present anxiety for some students.

The problem of meeting other people's expectations about your teaching can also be challenging. Mentors want you to fulfil the requirements of the teaching experience. Class teachers want you to provide the best for their children. Head teachers want you to be of benefit to their schools. Tutors want you to meet the college expectations. Somewhere in the middle of it all is *you*, with your own hopes, beliefs and aspirations about teaching. You have to make sure that you are not disorientated in your attempt to please everyone, and end up pleasing no-one. During a FASE, it is difficult to avoid the feeling that your every word and move is being scrutinised. The more quickly you can adopt a professional and business-like approach to the task of teaching, the quicker others will come to express confidence in your ability to teach.

The classroom itself may impose additional strains. Some classrooms are small and heave with bodies, furniture, learning materials and clutter, hindering ease of movement and creating logistical problems. Others are poorly designed and require a lot of creative thinking from the teacher to make the best use of what is available. Even the best designed classrooms have to be organised, resourced, and managed. Whatever type of classroom you are placed in you will have to make the best of the situation, buckle down to work, and stay positive.

BUSY MENTORS, BUSY TEACHERS

There are many demands made of mentors outside their immediate classroom work, such as being pleasant and cheery with teacher colleagues and students at a time when they are coping with their own teaching responsibilities. Strains occur as they try to fit in small but important tasks during break times while trying to snatch a drink and answer your queries at the same time. Most mentors volunteer to help students because they enjoy the challenge and rewards, not because of extra pay or incentives. They have to cope with extra meetings, paperwork and responsibility for observing students teach and giving advice and feedback. The work of mentoring is not only a highly skilled one, it also makes heavy time and emotional demands on those teachers. Your appreciative remarks will help mentors to feel that all the effort is worthwhile.

Every teacher is a busy teacher. They use a lot of energy when they address the class, offer explanations, deal with incidents and move about the room responding to various needs. Regular use of the voice at a variety of pitches and tones for different occasions is physically tiring. The intensity of maintaining a close relationship with a number of children at the same time absorbs energy and can lead to fatigue.

Other demands upon teachers are less obvious. For instance, teachers have to keep a close eye on the clock and make sure they start and end lessons on time. Although it would sometimes be a relief to end a lesson early if things are not progressing well, or continue long after the appointed time if things are flourishing, it is not possible within the bounds of normal school life. On some occasions children are called out of the class at different times throughout the day for recorder practices, health checks, photographs, dental appointments, and so on. While time constraints increase the need to prepare a lesson that will fit snugly into the allotted timetable space, this is difficult to achieve when planning a single lesson because it is not possible to predict interruptions and the pace at which children will work. Time pressures sometimes result in a frantic rush to fit everything in before the end of a session. Wiser teachers will tell you that it is better to leave some things for another time rather than hurry to include them because they were in the original lesson plan. However, there are occasions when it is important to complete the lesson in a single session, notably when using specialist facilities or equipment that has been booked for the purpose.

All teachers have meetings to attend, records to complete and planning to do. In your enthusiasm to ask for help and guidance, it is important to be sensitive to the other pressures and demands that the class teacher and mentor have to face daily.

Although it is quite common for mentors and class teachers to work non-stop throughout the day, this is generally unwise as it creates the conditions for ill-health. In reality, all school staff have to be prepared to face days when there seems to be insufficient time to breathe!

Priorities

In the need to manage time effectively, good lesson preparation is essential. Poor preparation not only adversely affects the children, but has serious consequences for the teacher:

POOR PREPARATION ➔ POOR QUALITY OF TEACHING-AND-LEARNING

POOR QUALITY OF TEACHING-AND-LEARNING ➔ ADDITIONAL STRESS

ADDITIONAL STRESS ➔ REDUCED ABILITY TO COPE

REDUCED ABILITY TO COPE ➔ INCREASED LIKELIHOOD OF EXHAUSTION

INCREASED LIKELIHOOD OF EXHAUSTION ➔ POOR PREPARATION . . .

Teaching is tiring, but it is also exhilarating when things go well. Sensible preparation and resulting good quality lessons are the most effective way of dealing with tiredness and raising your spirits.

MODELLING

As you meet different teachers and mentors in various schools, and evaluate their attitudes and abilities, take account of the following points:

No teacher is a perfect role model

However much they are good at their jobs, there will be areas of their teaching which are less successful than others. In fact, the best teachers are usually the most willing to admit that they never stop learning. However much you admire particular teachers, they all have their limitations. Part of your task as a trainee is to draw from their example and weave it into your own teaching, rather than attempting to replicate their approach.

A teacher is usually better under certain circumstances

A wonderful reception class teacher may struggle with eight year-olds. The brilliant junior PE teacher may be overwhelmed by rising-fives. The teacher who uses group work superbly well may be less effective with whole class approaches. You, too, will find yourself more at ease in certain situations, but you should avoid becoming inflexible. After all, your next teaching practice or first job may be very different from your current school experience.

Teachers tend to concentrate on the things they are good at

Sometimes a teacher will expect more from you than they can offer themselves. This is simply a reflection of the fact that teachers always hope that students will bring fresh insights into the teaching situation. Some teachers spend the minimum time possible on certain aspects of the curriculum or subject because they don't enjoy them or feel particularly competent to teach them. During your training you need to be competent in every curriculum area, and expert in at least one of them.

Teachers have their own priorities and beliefs

One teacher may shout to control the children; another may use well rehearsed hand signals to indicate what should be happening. One teacher may encourage collaborative problem-solving; another may spend a lot of time teaching from the front. One teacher may chat informally to children; another may insist upon maintaining a distance. Your admiration for teachers does not mean that you have to agree with everything they say and

REMEMBER: when you are a qualified teacher, students working in your classroom will be inclined to model themselves on you!

do. As you begin to develop your own educational philosophy, you will certainly find that a teacher's priorities are not always identical to your own. During school experience you have to learn to strike a balance between adopting the classroom procedures and teaching techniques preferred by the teacher, and developing your own strategies.

STAFF MEMBERSHIP

Life in school is not just about preparing and teaching lessons. It involves becoming part of the wider community. Much that you do is open to scrutiny by a variety of audiences: children, teaching staff, ancillary staff, secretary, parents, visitors. The way that you dress, behave, approach people, listen to others, respond to advice, laugh, smile, apply yourself to the job and persevere, will all be noted. Students who spend their time giggling and behaving immaturely will be treated with contempt by the regular staff, even if their classroom work is satisfactory. Similarly, students who arrive at the last minute, who are casual about their appearance, and who make little effort to be friendly and cheerful in the staffroom and around the school, are unlikely to win the hearts and minds of fellow workers. Parents, too, notice how students speak to their children and express their care, how they conduct themselves and respond to their comments and questions.

Being a teacher involves more than classroom activity; it requires the development of an attitude which indicates that you are worthy of respect and being treated like a teacher. It pays to remember that even as a temporary and inexperienced staff member, there are clear expectations of your role and conduct by those around you.

Success as a teacher

Success in teaching is difficult to define, but if both you and the children are eager to come to school, enjoy learning and relate comfortably to one another, you are well on your way to finding success. Another measure of success as a teacher is to examine the progress that children make in their academic work and measure their improvement over a given time. For instance, improvements in hand writing, knowledge of scientific facts, and understanding of mathematical concepts, can all be measured. Some things cannot be measured – for example kindness, co-operation, willingness, empathy, creativity. In practice, your success will depend partly on your own sense of fulfilment and partly on how well children learn. Both of these depend upon the existence of positive classroom relationships and a stimulating learning environment.

THE FOUR PS

Four other factors influence the extent of your teaching success:

- **Planning and preparation**
- **Placement**
- **Personality**
- **Performance**

Planning and preparation

Planning and preparation of lessons provides the foundations for effective teaching. It needs to be closely matched with the children's ability, taking into account their previous learning. The class teacher will already have plans in place based on the agreed school curriculum policy, and your plans must fit in with them. Most students find that their lesson preparation improves as they get to know the children better and become familiar with their individual needs and abilities. Further information about planning and preparation can be found in Chapter 5.

Placement

Placement can make a big difference to your approach as school situations vary in a number of important respects.

SIZE

Primary schools can be so small that they are allowed only two teachers; or so large that they are bigger than some secondary schools. Small schools sometimes liaise closely with other nearby schools of similar size. Teachers in small schools need to be versatile and prepared to take on a broad range of responsibilities. Classes in smaller schools often contain children from several year groups. Sometimes a smaller school does not have its own large space for PE or drama, and the activities take place in village halls, playgrounds or even in a large classroom. Larger schools normally have better resources and there is greater opportunity for teachers to specialise. They tend to have at least one hall or large space for curriculum activities and for meal times. Classes tend to be composed of a single year group.

PUPILS

Some schools draw from large estates, others from widespread rural communities, with others from comfortable suburbia. Although it is tempting to imagine that schools in economically poor areas are the worst, this is not necessarily true. A lot depends upon the head teacher, the attitude of local parents and the community spirit existing in that district. Some schools in affluent areas can be uninspiring and discouraging places to work, both for children and staff. Some schools in the poorest areas can sparkle with life and vitality. Nevertheless, it is obvious that some children will come from homes that do not conform to the cheery, relaxed images frequently seen on the front of magazine covers or on our TV screens. There are also additional demands made by children whose home language is one other than English, those who are distressed or emotionally insecure, and those who have received little encouragement from home.

   You cannot alter the home circumstances, but you can take careful note of the way in which the school deals with these challenges, and determine for yourself to take a positive rather than a defeatist approach to your teaching. Children from a disadvantaged background are *doubly* disadvantaged if you have low expectations of them. Teachers in the best schools use their energies to find constructive ways to develop children's potential, rather than focus on their shortcomings. You should do the same.

STAFF

Most primary schools are welcoming and cheery, and the majority of the staff are good hearted. Some schools use teachers as specialists in different subjects; others allocate responsibilities based on year groups or staff groups. Increasingly, schools are utilising a range of adult helpers for different tasks: classroom assistants, parents, trainee nursery nurses and so on (Mills and Mills, 1995). Job sharing, use of specialist teachers not directly employed by the school (and for music perhaps) and exchange of teachers within the school for particular sessions (such as the teacher specialising in technology swopping with the teacher for swimming) are now commonplace. Although strict staff hierarchies rarely operate within primary schools, the head teacher is responsible for the school's performance and accountable to parents, governors and inspectors. As a student teacher, you will be playing your part in assisting the head teacher and staff with their demanding task of ensuring the maintenance of high achievement and a purposeful school environment.

ORGANISATION

This is sometimes the most distinguishing feature of all. You may teach a single age-range or several ages in the same class. Children may be divided by ability or in mixed ability groups. Classes may remain with a single teacher throughout the week or (in England and Wales especially at Key Stage 2) have different teachers for different subjects. Sometimes, groups of children may take turns with a specialist teacher for subjects such as Information Technology, reading, and language teaching. The school may contain a multiplicity of languages or a single one, and there may be particular procedures and approaches which take account of the ethnic backgrounds of the children. Some children may go to special classes to learn English as a second language, or to study their first language and associated customs in depth. Most teaching programmes incorporate blocks of time focusing upon particular religious festivals. Within individual classes the organisation will depend upon the age of the children and the preferences of the teacher.

Personality

Personality also plays an essential role in your success as a teacher. If you are enthusiastic, eager to learn, cool-headed, willing to take things in your stride and able to see the funny side of life, you stand a good chance of succeeding. Students with many different personalities can be effective practitioners; however, miserable pessimists with a sour attitude to life need not apply!

Performance

Performance in the classroom depends to a large extent upon knowing what you are doing, carrying it out wholeheartedly, and using the full range of your teaching skills. Successful students are like skilled drivers: they master the basic controls, steer the vehicle sensitively, vary the speed according to the conditions, anticipate problems and (most importantly) ensure that they control the vehicle (and not the other way around). Whatever the demands of your school experience, your overall success depends upon your willingness to learn quickly and respond to the conditions that you find in the school and classroom.

A large part of this book is concerned with ways to develop your classroom skills as a means of improving the quality of teaching and learning. In doing so, remember that your hard-working school mentor and class teacher will be as keen as anybody for you to prosper in your school experience.

CHAPTER 3

The School and Classroom Context

The classroom in use is a highly complex and fascinating system

(Proctor et al, 1995)

Imagine a situation in which athletes were told that they would be entered for a competition but were not allowed to know the location of the event or the names of the other contestants. Such an arrangement would be unthinkable. Before major events take place, participants need to spend time getting the feel of the venue, mentally rehearsing their ideas and strategies, and adjusting their approach to fit the situation.

KNOW YOUR SCHOOL

In the same way, students going into school to practise teaching need to know as much as they can about the particular circumstances of the school and class in which they are about to work. In this way, they stand more chance of making the best use of their time there. The quicker this information can be gathered, the more likely that the school experience will be a success.

The preliminary visit

Depending upon the precise nature of your school experience, most college departments arrange for you to make a *preliminary visit* to gain information about the school prior to the start of your time in school. It is important that you make good use of this time – for some students it can mean the difference between making a tentative or a positive beginning, between a high and low grade, or even between success and failure. The problem facing every student who is meeting a new school situation is to tune in to the way in which things function and all the associated 'dos' and 'do nots' that permanent staff understand but newcomers cannot possibly know. The more quickly this alignment takes place, the happier everyone will be and the greater chance you will have of making an impressive start. Teachers and mentors quickly notice and admire those students who attempt to fit in with the class and school routines. Even those students who have spent time in school doing other jobs (such as classroom assistant) have to make a substantial effort to learn the procedures and expectations associated with a particular school placement.

Placement schools

Every type of school which educates children at Key Stages 1 or 2 is deemed **primary**. Your host school is likely to fall into one of the following types:

- a *nursery* **school for children aged 3 and 4 years (a forerunner to formal primary education);**
- an *infant* **school (Key Stage 1) for children from 5 to 7 years (Reception, Year 1, Year 2);**
- a *first* **school (Key Stage 1 and the first part of Key Stage 2) for children from 5 to 8 or 9 years (Reception, Years 1, 2, 3 and, for 5-9 schools, Year 4);**
- a *primary* **school (ey Stages 1 and 2) for children from 5 to 11 years (Reception, Years 1-6);**
- a *middle* **school for children from 8 or 9 to 12 or 13 years (to include the early part of Key Stage 3 for Years 7 and 8);**
- a *high* **school for children from 12 to 16 years;**
- a *secondary* **school from 11 to 16 or 11 to 18 years.**

An infant, first or primary school may also have a nursery class or unit attached to the school. Many primary schools also have informal links with playgroups or local nursery units, and the children feed from them into the main school reception class at the start of the term in which they will have their fifth birthday.

Reception classes

Children in the reception class (known as *rising fives*) normally remain in the class until the end of the academic year, when they transfer to their new class (Year 1), though sometimes the summer term entrants stay with the same teacher for the following year. As beginners enter school at different times throughout this reception year, the reception class grows increasingly larger. This means that although in September the reception class is sometimes very small, by the end of the year it can become three times the size:

- *September* **reception class: composed of children who will reach their fifth birthday before January**
- *January* **reception class: composed of children who started in September (now five years old) plus the new entrants who will reach their fifth birthday before April**
- *April* **reception class: composed of children who started in September and in April, plus the new entrants who will reach their fifth birthday before the end of August**

With the current expansion of nursery education for four year-olds, there may be a change in the way that reception classes are organised. Some smaller schools combine their reception classes with the Year 1 class; the teacher then has to cope with a situation in which children span two Year groups. Once children reach five years of age, they can be introduced to the National Curriculum programme. Some schools use the reception class as a time for developing basic skills through *Areas of Learning*. In addition to facts about their progress in aspects of English and maths, Areas of Learning for young children include information about their personal and social development, creativity and knowledge and understanding of the world. The reception class is an important time in which positive attitudes to learning are formed in preparation for more formal schooling from Year 1 onwards. If you teach a reception class, you will be kept very busy throughout the day as you cope with the multitude of demands and needs of children who, though unused to school life, have already had nearly five years experience of life outside.

Knowing the school

Once you have been allocated to a school, it is important to consider the numerous practical considerations facing you. The remainder of this chapter refers to aspects of school life that need to be considered during your time in school. For convenience, they are divided into six areas:

- **General**
- **Daily procedures**
- **Relationships**
- **Curriculum**
- **Classroom organisation**
- **Teaching approach**

Although you cannot possibly expect to grasp everything immediately, the advice below provides a framework for action during your time in school.

GENERAL

Travelling to and from school

Many students have little choice about their placement school, though some colleges make allowances for students with particular circumstances such as family responsibilities. Other colleges expect students to make their own arrangements for accommodation and transport for teaching practices.

It is important for you to be clear about how you are going to reach school each day. It is a fortunate student who can walk to school; most rely on lifts, college mini-buses or public transport. Even if you have a car, parking space may be restricted on the school site, especially in inner-city areas. Whatever your method of travel, you need to take into account the practicalities of carrying bags of books, large sheets and heavy teaching practice files. The short walk up the hill can feel like a marathon if 30 exercise books or a bag full of history artefacts have to be hauled along as well. Similarly, the 10 minute drive into school when carrying out a trial run on a lazy Sunday afternoon can extend to half an hour in Monday morning rush-hour traffic. A two-bus journey followed by a long walk to school may be manageable in the morning but extract the last dregs of residual energy following a tough day. These factors are part of your school experience and you need to be aware of them.

The school day

To ensure that you monitor your use of time, it is helpful to sub-divide the school day into phases (see Figure 3.1 below):

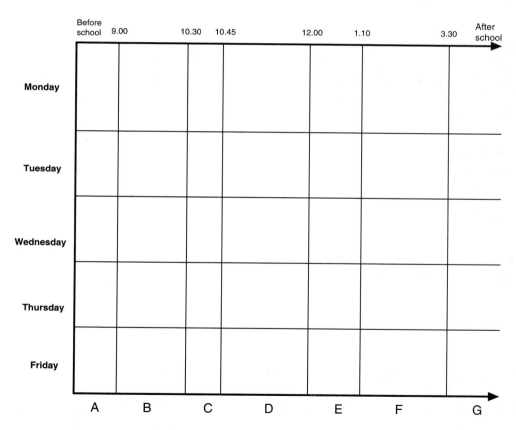

A. Arrival and preparation time

B. Direct contact time (1)

C. Morning break

D. Direct contact time (2)

E. Lunch break

F. Direct contact time (3)

G. After school preparation, marking, and classroom enhancement time

Figure 3.1 Daily overview proforma

As a general rule it is worth arriving at school a minimum of 20 minutes before the start of the day. Despite the fact that some teachers occasionally arrive just before the bell, the majority will be at work in good time to allow for any setting up or brief discussions with colleagues about the day ahead. These early morning encounters are important. They allow teachers to rehearse their ideas with another teacher, gain moral support and exchange pleasantries that are an essential part of the team-building process. You may misinterpret these casual encounters before school (and during breaks) as nothing more than friendship bonding; in fact, they go much deeper than this and form an essential element of professional life.

REMEMBER: Teachers notice at what time you arrive and leave school, and how you spend it.

The time a teacher spends after school often depends upon the particular circumstances: one teacher may leave early because of a family commitment or attending a meeting; others will stay until six o'clock each evening because they do not have other demands upon their time outside school. There is no merit in working excessively long hours for the sake of doing so, but there are times when showing a willingness to remain behind after school to pin up pictures, mark some books or talk to teachers is well worth the extra effort. If you have to leave promptly because of travel arrangements, make sure that you tell the teacher why you cannot stay and don't assume that she knows instinctively. Perhaps you can make a special effort to use a lunch break for those extra tasks instead.

The school building

Learn about the school's geography, not merely because you may get lost but because it helps you to feel part of the school and not need to rely upon others to guide you. The particular context – buildings, grounds, facilities – plays an important part in the learning process and the social interactions that take place regularly in school. For instance, bold welcome signs on the front entrance, clearly marked direction arrows and an attractive foyer, all point to a school in which the community and visitors are viewed positively. Well decorated classrooms, carpeted corridors, resource areas and well-stocked libraries give messages about the school's priorities.

DO YOU KNOW the name and location of the school nurse or first-aider?

Find out where the children's toilets are located and which toilets are allocated to which age groups, especially in a larger school in which there is often more than one block. Make sure you know how the children reach the toilets from your classroom and the logistics of allowing them to leave the classroom to do so during the day. Similarly, make sure that you know where to find the head teacher's room, medical room or sick bay, telephone, hall, dining room and PE/games equipment.

Security

It is regrettable that due to increasing concerns about the safety of pupils and staff, schools have become more wary about the presence of strangers in the building. Many schools operate a signing-in procedure and issue visitors' badges. Others have reduced the number of access doors. A few larger schools have introduced security cameras or security guards.

However onerous it may be to comply with the procedures, it is important that you co-operate and, together with every other responsible adult, maintain a cautious watch for any suspicious activity. Remember that schools are all trying to maintain a balance between openness and taking sensible precautions.

> **HAVE YOU THOUGHT ABOUT** what you should do if you see someone suspicious in or around the building?

Referring to staff

The teacher may be called 'Tib' by her friends in the shelter of the staff room; however, to walk into the classroom calling out 'Tib, Tib' will sound more like a cat-call than addressing a professional. It is better to stick with the teacher's formal name, especially in front of the children, unless otherwise requested. Always use the *head teacher's* formal name rather than an informal one, even if the regular staff use the latter. Courtesy and professional good manners are important in maintaining good relations in school and they need to be cultivated.

> **TEACHERS are as impressed by** your attitude to adults as they are to your attitude to children.

Ancillary staff

Take the trouble to learn the names of ancillary staff with whom you work regularly. Classroom assistants and voluntary helpers do not always receive the recognition that they deserve, so make sure that you gain an ally by offering them the same courtesy you give the teacher.

You also need to find out when any extra adult help is available during the week, or you might plan something on the mistaken assumption that while you are teaching clay work there is someone to assist children with their needle craft. To ensure that you are not caught out, mark on your weekly plan when the classroom assistant or helper is available, and check the arrangements with them at the start of each week.

Schools are places for grown-ups as well as children; the most successful schools are characterised by teamwork and co-operation, involving the full range of adult workers. It also pays to get to know ancillary staff such as the caretaker and secretary, and the teachers and helpers in adjacent classrooms.

Resources

School-wide resources such as access to library, archives and consumables form an important element of school life. Ask the class teacher what is available within the school and what you need to bring into school for yourself. Schools vary in the latitude they give to students to help themselves to consumables such as paper and card. Similarly, there may be resources such as books and visual aids for use by staff but denied to students, either because it is felt that students use them up too quickly or because the resources have been allocated to staff in advance and there is little to spare. It is very likely that class teachers will have their own classroom supplies, in which case you will normally be able to use them. Paper and (especially) pencils need to be guarded and cherished in school; they sometimes seem to disappear down a deep hole over the term and most teachers jealously watch over their supply. It is only when these basic commodities run short due to careless distribution or use that you realise how much work in school depends on them.

Take great care over the use of artefacts and equipment. It can ruin a beautiful friendship if you are casual with the teacher's best-loved thermometers and they gently slide off the table when your back is turned. If possible, bring in a few interesting items of your own for the classroom as a gesture of goodwill.

FIND OUT where resources are kept and the system for borrowing them.

Most schools have a photocopier. A few head teachers allow free access by all staff and students, but the majority insist upon exercising some control over this part of the expenditure. Some schools give teachers a limited budget which, once used, is not replenished; others have code numbers for every teacher to use; yet others simply ask for a log book to be filled in. Check the school system for photocopying.

Dress code

Some head teachers are very fussy about the way in which children dress; some have particular ideas about the way staff dress; most are concerned with both. In the majority of schools, teachers are expected to come to school looking tidy but not over-dressed. If you dress conventionally during the first few days, you can modify your style as appropriate when it becomes clear whether business suits or boiler suits are acceptable in the school. It can come as quite a shock to an over-cautious student to go in to school dressed formally, only to be confronted by a head teacher attired in a pair of shorts and a baseball cap! Nevertheless, it pays to be conservative and put fashion consciousness aside. Common sense dictates that clothes should be worn appropriate to the situation (particularly the correct footwear for games activities).

REMEMBER: Children and parents pay close attention to the clothes that teachers wear.

Parents in school

Parents are often used in school to support the learning process (through hearing readers, for instance) or offering practical support (such as mending library books). Your school will have an established policy for parents in school and the tasks that they are encouraged to do. In practice, class teachers tend to negotiate directly with individual parents about their role.

While you are in school, you should be careful about the impression that you give to parents:

a) because they will watch you and talk to their friends about you;

b) because their children may be members of your class;

c) because your behaviour might affect the class teacher's reputation.

It is important that you do not give parents *detailed* information about their children's progress or raise sensitive issues with them without the presence and approval of the class teacher. Even your general comments will be taken seriously by parents and children, so beware of making casual remarks in an unguarded moment.

DAILY PROCEDURES

There are important procedures and routines of which you must become aware if you are to assist the teacher in the smooth-running of the classroom. Small but significant procedures can make a large difference to your confidence in dealing with the classroom situation – for instance by knowing the time and place of assemblies or acts of worship. If the school is multi-faith, find out about the assembly arrangements for different groups of children.

There are also daily events such as taking home spelling lists, reading books and homework. There are trays that have to be tidied, library books that have to be changed, plants that have to be watered, rainfall that has to be measured. Some class teachers like to bring the children together at certain times during the day for specific purposes involving sharing, discussing, celebrating and telling stories.

Pay attention to the system for keeping the attendance register, dinner money collection, absence notes, late arrivals to school, and the procedure for giving children letters to take home. Even if you are not directly responsible, it is good to keep yourself informed.

Once you begin your teaching experience it is essential to abide by regular specified times, in particular:

- **start of school**
- **break times**
- **going home time.**

No teacher who teaches very young children will permit them to go home alone if they are normally met by an adult. Sometimes a child is only allowed to go home with one designated adult and no other (for instance when parents have separated there may be agreed access to the children.) Although it is difficult to monitor this arrangement, especially when you are new to the school, it is important to be vigilant and try to remember any exceptional circumstances which might affect the arrangements.

Unexpected events

The school day takes many twists and turns, and cannot always be predictably slotted into neat categories. Pay attention to those events and unusual occurrences that might influence your day once you begin teaching.

Timetabling for designated spaces

Unlike secondary schools, many primary schools do not have strict time-tabling other than for set activities requiring specialist facilities. In particular, time for use of the hall is normally allocated to different classes as fairly as possible. Occasionally, a school is short of space and has to utilise the hall for a time as an additional classroom area. In the run up to special occasions, the hall may be out of action due to rehearsals for a play, a festival or an event. This can be frustrating if it interferes with your teaching, but such events are part of school life and it is best to know in advance about interruptions than to discover it half an hour before. If your hall time is immediately before or after lunch, you may find that the session is shorter due to the need to set out or clear away dinner tables.

Other activities that may be specifically time-tabled include the use of the games' field, computer area, music area, swimming pool and resource area. If you are involved in any 'outside' activity (such as rounders), find out the procedure for wet days.

Health and Safety

Schools are much more safety conscious than was once the case. Three aspects are significant:

1) fire drill and assembly points
2) children's personal safety
3) adults' personal safety.

1) FIRE DRILL AND ASSEMBLY POINTS

All schools have to carry out a regular fire drill to ensure that the procedures for evacuating the building are well rehearsed. All schools have regular fire practices and the teacher will expect you to play your part and have a clear idea about what to do should the need arise. Check on the classroom wall for the regulations and make sure you know the location of the assembly point outside the building.

2) CHILDREN'S PERSONAL SAFETY

The children's personal safety is obviously of paramount importance. Young children will sometimes put themselves in peril due to their over-enthusiasm or lack of experience. Common sense plays a major part in safeguarding them, but their proper training in the use of tools, adequate supervision during physical activities, and insistence upon basic standards of behaviour will normally prevent accidents occurring. If there are children in the class who are prone to particular ailments (notably fits and allergies), it is important to know the symptoms which indicate that something is wrong, and the correct procedures to follow (such as who to contact and what to do in an emergency). Children who receive additional classroom support owing to their special physical needs are normally cared for by the assistant; however, you still need to be aware of what to do should the assistant be absent or unavailable. Medicines are normally not allowed in classrooms and you must never administer any while you are in school. Children who suffer from asthma and use inhalers are increasingly responsible for their own medication, though you may be asked to monitor its usage. Take advice from the class teacher if in doubt, and do not exceed your responsibilities.

3) ADULTS' PERSONAL SAFETY

Your own safety is also important. For instance, it is essential to wear the correct shoes for the job. High heels are particularly unsuitable for school. If you have to spend time outside avoid excessive heat or cold, especially standing shivering while the children run around during a games' session. Never attempt to climb onto furniture or up ladders. Take great care over the use of gun staplers. Teaching practice is already sufficiently demanding without adding the burden of avoidable illness or injury.

A school's greatest resource is a fresh teacher.

You are also more likely to prosper on your practice if you maintain a regular sleep pattern. There is little merit in staying up in to the early hours to complete a task, however essential it seems to be, if it leaves you feeling jaded and grumpy the following day.

After-school and extra-curricular activities

Most schools run extra clubs and activities which either enhance the regular teaching (such as a computer or drama club) or provide a completely different learning experience (such as a chess club). You may be asked to assist with one of these activities by your class teacher or, if you are perceived as having some expertise in a particular area, by another teacher. Generally, it is worth responding positively to the invitation to help, providing it does not detract from your regular task of teaching. Teachers usually value your assistance and give you a lot of credit for making the effort to get involved. Nevertheless, there is no point in having a wonderful time running a lunchtime cross country club if you arrive late for the afternoon session in a state of exhaustion and disarray!

Personal possessions in school

All children love to bring in some personal items to show their friends or teacher. Many schools have rules to ensure that this process does not get out of hand. If children do bring in toys or other personal items, some teachers have a lockable drawer in which they can be safely left. It is a sad fact of life that if property is unguarded, there is always the possibility of theft. If a child asks you where an item should be left or whether you will take care of it, be sure to follow the accepted classroom procedures.

RELATIONSHIPS

A lot has been written about the importance of a good team spirit, co-operation and collaboration between members of staff, and the need for positive, mutually respectful relationships between children and adults. Your placement school will promote qualities of fairness, equal opportunities and a positive ethos, both in the classroom and staffroom (Lawrence, 1996). You will be expected to play your part in furthering them.

The classroom

Recognise that for many children, the classroom holds a special place in their hearts. Although a small number of children find school tedious and would prefer to be elsewhere, the majority enjoy meeting their friends and sharing learning experiences through formal lessons, extra-curricular activities and informal opportunities to have fun together. As you work alongside them in the classroom, bear in mind that you are entering a social system involving a network of alliances, mutual support, rivalries and self-discovery. The older the children, the more sophisticated the system becomes. It pays to be aware of what is happening and to take account of it in your teaching.

Sharing together

Many schools encourage children to show mutual responsibility and encouragement by gathering in a circle with the teacher to share ideas, celebrate good news and make kind remarks about one another. If handled sensitively, these occasions can benefit children and create a happy atmosphere, conducive to learning.

Classroom order

Carefully observe the class teacher's approach to maintaining control and ensure that you are familiar with any classroom rules. Watch for instances in which the teacher negotiates with the children and when she is inflexible; when she allows children to explain and when she rebukes them; when the tone of voice is natural and when it is severe. Use the class teacher as a model for your own approach, but do not expect to emulate her success immediately. Pay particularly close attention to the teacher's use of classroom rewards, such as team points, marbles in a jar, stars and stickers. Remember that rewards can be for *good behaviour* as much as for high standards of work. Details about your own role in maintaining classroom order can be found in Chapter 7.

CURRICULUM

The hidden curriculum

We have seen that the curriculum consists of the necessary content of the school's formal learning programme and the learning which takes place, whether deliberate or unplanned. Many head teachers consider that a positive and encouraging school ethos is an essential element of the curriculum, as it instils in both children and staff a desire to ask questions, investigate and take risks in learning. This positive atmosphere is sometimes referred to as the *hidden curriculum*; perhaps a more accurate description would be *what this school stands for*. Although the hidden curriculum is not easily defined, you will know it when you feel it! However, most of the following section deals principally with things to look for in the *formally* taught curriculum.

What you will teach

The most important subjects that you will teach are English (especially Reading and Writing) and Maths (especially Number work). Your school may use schemes or systematic approaches for the core subjects, especially in Maths. Most teachers do not rely totally on commercially produced materials, but produce their own, taking into account the particular needs of the children.

READING

Take careful account of the teacher's approach to reading: use of published book schemes, phonics teaching, methods of selecting books, record-keeping, sending books home, assessment of progress, use of the library, quiet reading times, shared or paired reading times, and so on. Children with reading difficulties may receive regular extra support during special times during the day.

Pay attention to the way teachers or assistants recognise and correct errors in reading, when they allow the child to read on, and what is recorded about the reading.

It is likely that there will be close links established between reading, writing and spelling. The teacher may draw up spelling lists or use the children's own work as a basis for identifying key words. For further details about teaching reading, see pages 96 to 103.

WRITING

Most schools have a standard approach to handwriting. Writing development is sometimes closely structured with a lot of teacher intervention, or sometimes children are given the freedom to express themselves regardless of the quality and content of the work. Older children tend to write an independent draft version which is subsequently improved with teacher help.

In most classes, children are introduced to a range of writing: reporting events, recounting stories and personal circumstances, make-believe, describing processes (for example in a science experiment) and enquiring. Find out what types of writing your class is used to doing. Perhaps you will have opportunity to use similar ideas or introduce variations, such as letters to famous people, contributions to debate (about local issues, for instance), writing to children in other classes, short plays, and so on.

Most classes for children aged 7 to 11 have formal lessons about the structure of language and English grammar. These lessons are sometimes followed by formally structured sessions using worksheets, booklets or published schemes.

NUMERACY

This is such an important area of learning that you need to pay special attention to the class teacher's approach to teaching it. Not only will the children be involved in activities which assist them to count, read and write numbers and recognise number patterns, but also to work flexibly, use resources and record findings in different ways. Some aspects of number work deal with algebraic concepts, especially for 7 to 11 year-olds. Look out for the way in which mathematical understanding of number is applied in practical ways, the sorts of questions that are raised and how children approach problem solving. You also need to be aware of the *language* used in conveying mathematical thought and the thinking which influences lessons. More able children will work with different methods of computation and mathematical operations. All children will use calculators to explore number structures, work out answers to real problems, and have access to computers for setting up and accessing a database of information.

In some classes, there is a heavy reliance upon the set mathematics text; in others, teachers choose to be more independent and produce their own materials, especially maths games (Hewett, 1984). Younger and less able children have to rely heavily upon counting aids to carry out calculations; older and more able children use more mental calculations and are likely to be more ambitious in the strategies they employ for solving problems. Although numeracy is not the only area of maths, it is by far the most important and will probably receive priority attention from the class teacher.

Topics and themes

In addition to teaching English and Maths, you may be required to participate in the teaching of a topic or theme during your time in school. If so, you should find out how far advanced it is or whether you are expected to introduce it. For instance, a History theme (such as 'Invaders and Settlers') may be focusing on the Romans in Britain; you need to know exactly which elements of knowledge, skills and understanding have been covered up to the point you arrive in school. Otherwise you may make unwarranted assumptions about the children's progress. If you begin your teaching experience a few weeks into a term, it is likely that the class teacher has already established the pattern of teaching; if you *introduce* the subject, you have more control over your teaching strategies. Even if the class teacher has given you a full picture of progress to date, you will need to spend a few days working in the classroom before children's learning patterns become clear. Remember that if you have a preliminary visit some weeks before the start of the placement, the children will have moved on in their learning by the time you arrive. It is useful to contact the class teacher a few days before the start if you have any uncertainties about the children's progress or what areas have been covered.

Broadcasts

Some schools make considerable use of radio and TV broadcasts which are seen live or recorded and seen later. Find out what resources are used to introduce the programme topic and how the broadcast is used in the children's learning. Some broadcasts have accompanying work sheets; you should note how they are used and evaluate their effectiveness in supporting the rest of the teaching.

Out-of-school

Make sure that you ask the teacher about forthcoming educational visits. It is important to discover the range of educational resources within easy walking distance of the classroom. Some schools have conservation zones, woodlands and wild areas. Some have buildings of particular architectural design, ideal for supporting work in art, shape and design technology. You will not normally be asked to organise a trip away from school unless this is your final FASE. Even if you intend to stay within the school boundary, check the school rules for taking children out of the classroom and plan accordingly.

Homework

Over the past few years there has been a resurgence of interest in the use of homework as a means of extending learning and increasing the partnership element between school and home. Your school will have a policy for homework; either it will not be in use as a formal part of the curriculum or guidelines will exist over the way it must be used. If homework is used, take note of how often it is given, the form it takes, and how it is monitored. Some schools use reading practice as the mainstay of homework for younger children. Other schools ask the children to find out about different topics by using the local library or other sources. Generally, the older the children, the more likely that formal homework will be set.

Assessment, Recording and Reporting

The process of Assessment, Recording and Reporting (AR and R) is one that is relevant to every teacher. Your placement school will probably have an overall *marking policy*, but the age of children determines the way in which it is interpreted by the teachers. Class teachers may have their own system of assessing children's work, giving appropriate feedback and recording progress. At different times in the year, this information will be conveyed to parents orally and in written form. As an inexperienced student, you will probably be expected to keep a limited number of records, including those for reading. Check your college documentation carefully for the minimum requirements and liaise with the class teacher about which system you should employ.

CLASSROOM ORGANISATION

An important element of your experience in school involves a close observation of how the class teacher organises the children's learning experiences:

1) Organisation of the main teaching area
2) Organisation of additional work areas
3) Organisation of resources
4) Organisation of display space.

1) Organisation of the main teaching area

Make a plan view of the room, noting the position of tables, chairs, boards, books, displays and special areas. Note any changes in the pattern of arrangement which occur during the day. For instance, whether tables are pushed together for certain activities, furniture cleared for drama, painting easels pulled into position, computer trolleys wheeled to a different location. There are two reasons for noting these details:

- **it forces you to familiarise yourself with the classroom layout and**
- **it encourages you to think about the implications for your teaching.**

NEVER alter the room without fully consulting the teacher, who may then decide to consult the children before agreeing changes.

The second point is important. The classroom layout is organised to facilitate learning and ensure that children can move about easily. For example, the sand and water area is placed away from major routeways (so that children don't get splashed) and on a properly tiled space (so that the floor does not get slippery and any mess is easy to clear up). Similarly, if any electrical equipment is in use, there must be access to sockets without the need for trailing wires. The location of doors, windows and heaters will also restrict the positioning of furniture. Find an opportunity to talk to your class teacher about the room organisation. He may point out features that you had not noticed, or may invite you to make small changes once you begin teaching.

2) Organisation of additional work areas

Find out about the use of activity areas outside the main classroom. Many schools have extra work space available, including corridors, adjoining rooms, craft areas and even cloakrooms. Modern school buildings may have specially wide corridors in which computers, book displays and large-scale construction equipment are kept. The class teacher will have a system for allowing children to use these additional resources, so you need to be familiar with the system to ensure fairness and continuity. The availability of extra space is often beneficial as it allows children to have more room to work and can generate a more pleasant working environment. However, there are logistical factors to consider, including difficulties in monitoring children's progress and ensuring that no-one misuses their freedom. See Chapter 5 for further details about classroom layouts and their impact upon teaching.

3) Organisation of resources

Classroom resources include consumables, equipment and books. The *consumables* are the paper, pencils, exercise books, paint and glue that need regular replenishing. The *equipment* includes everything else apart from published books. The *books* consist of three main kinds:

- **those specifically to provide information, such as encyclopaedias;**
- **those designated part of a structured, sequential reading scheme;**
- **fiction books which occupy library shelves for free choice by children.**

Note the importance that the class teacher attaches to the correct use of resources, returning everything to its proper place, and ensuring that all children have fair and appropriate access to the more appealing items such as science equipment and computers.

4) Organisation of display space

Some teachers place a lot of emphasis upon display work and encourage the children to produce murals, paintings, sketches, news items and other visually attractive products that can be used for this purpose. Many teachers teach children to mount their own work, contribute items for table displays and produce large, colourful labels. Clarify the teacher's expectations, and ask advice about the time and procedures required to produce a display.

It is not advisable to take responsibility for too much display work, unless a major part of your school experience is for this specific purpose, as the time it takes can detract from other important tasks. If you are uncertain about the value of a display, use the same criteria that you would use before preparing a lesson:

- **What contribution does it make to the children's education?**
- **What will the children learn as a result?**
- **What evidence does it provide you about standards of work and teacher expectations?**

There will be classroom procedures for dealing with completed and uncompleted work. For instance, there may be drying racks for paintings and specially designated trays for work that requires marking. A lot of classroom work is carried over into future sessions; if the uncompleted work is carelessly handled, the results are a source of annoyance when the activity is recommenced.

TEACHING APPROACH

Teachers use a variety of teaching approaches: dividing the class into ability or friendship groups, whole class activities, direct teaching from the front of the class, discovery methods in which children find out for themselves, use of visual aids, invited guests, outings and so on. Note when these approaches are used, and how effective they appear to be in involving children in their learning as well as fostering a purposeful classroom atmosphere.

General behaviour

One of the most difficult aspects of class management to comprehend are the rules governing behaviour. It is demoralising for you to allow a child to do something, only to hear the class teacher asking: 'What are you doing over there, Henry Timms?' and hear his defensive reply that 'Miss told me I could'. The more you can be aware of what is acceptable, the stronger your authority as a teacher will become. Some classrooms are remarkably free and easy; children seem to move around at will; other classrooms are more rigid and children have to seek permission to change place. Most teachers allow freedom of movement, providing it does not detract from the work in hand. Some occasions (such as a story time or a whole class explanation) demand that every child is sitting still. Other times (such as a science workshop) may call for flexibility of movement. In practice, every teacher needs to make a large number of decisions daily about the things that they are prepared to allow. In the early days of the practice, it is useful for you to be able to say that 'Mr Godfrey does not allow you to do that, and neither shall I'.

Special needs

Most classes contain some children who have learning problems. Some children have special needs that disadvantage them but are insufficiently serious to justify extra resources. Such children are likely to work slowly, get bored easily and rely heavily on adult support. It is important to find out who these children are and what role (if any) you are to take in teaching them. A small number of children have learning problems (sometimes coupled with poor behaviour) that are more severe and Individual Education Plans (IEPs) have been established for them. These children sometimes go out of the main classroom for specialist teaching from the designated teacher. Others have a support assistant to give individual tuition or help with general discipline.

Finally

You may have little or considerable choice about where you are placed in school. Either way, by carrying out careful observations, asking the class teacher a range of intelligent questions and carefully reflecting about the circumstances of class and school life, you will give yourself a firm base from which to spring once your teaching experience begins in earnest.

Regardless of your school situation, you need to have a good grasp of the content and requirements of National Curriculum documentation. The following chapter will help you to start the process.

CHAPTER 4

The National Curriculum

The National Curriculum is not a strait jacket. It provides for greater clarity and precision about what should be taught, while enabling schools to retain flexibility about how they organise their teaching.

(Cox and Sanders, 1994)

The school curriculum can be defined in different ways: the sum of all the subject content taught in a school; the knowledge, skills and understanding required by children; formally taught lessons; formal and informal learning; everything that is taught and learned in school. Most student teachers are concerned with the content of the prescribed national curriculum (for example the National Curriculum for England, Wales and Northern Ireland), but it is important to realize that your positive response to children's spontaneous reactions, interests and fascination with life is an important element of extending children's knowledge. Not everything that is useful for life is found in a curriculum document, however carefully it is constructed. Your formal teaching should also take account of the latent creativity and wonder that is found in every child. Indeed, the more that your formal teaching utilises the child's curiosity and enthusiasm, the more effective your teaching is likely to become. This chapter is primarily concerned with the National Curriculum for England and Wales.

THE NATIONAL CURRICULUM FOR ENGLAND AND WALES

There are many important aspects of pupils' learning, such as the development of social skills, independence, collaboration and co-operation that need to be taken into account when teaching. However, as the National Curriculum programme is an entitlement for every child aged five years and over, it must strongly influence the direction of lesson preparation. As a trainee teacher you will need to master the basic vocabulary associated with the National Curriculum and become thoroughly familiar with details of the documents and your own single subject, as well as having a sound working knowledge of the other subjects and Religious Education. The National Curriculum is divided into four Key Stages for pupils in maintained schools:

- *Key Stage 1* (KS1) for pupils aged 5 to 7 years (Year groups 1 and 2)
- *Key Stage 2* (KS2) for pupils aged 7 to 11 years (Year groups 3, 4, 5 and 6);
- *Key Stage 3* (KS3) for pupils aged 11 to 14 years (Year groups 7, 8 and 9);
- *Key Stage 4* (KS4) for pupils aged 14 to 16 (Year groups 10 and 11).

Conventional primary schools (5 to 11 years) cover Key Stages 1 and 2. Infant schools (5 to 7 years) cover Key Stage 1. Junior schools (7 to 11 years) cover Key Stage 2. Since the introduction of a national curriculum, more schools have become conventional primaries (5 to 11) to avoid the complications associated with crossing key stages.

As the National Curriculum is so important, you need to have a clear picture of the content and format of the different subjects at the Key Stages. Although it is common for students on their first teaching experience to concentrate on a limited range of subjects (especially Maths and English), many lessons cross subject barriers. In particular, literacy, numeracy and study skills (such as using reference books) are relevant to the majority of lessons. Although familiarity with the National Curriculum will not, of itself, make you a good teacher, it will give you confidence and save you time in lesson preparation.

The details of the National Curriculum documentation is similar for England and Wales, though the latter takes account of the Welsh language. The National Curriculum (1995) from the DfE (published by HMSO) contains the full text, but the following information will help you to find your way around it.

Programmes of Study

Each National Curriculum subject sets out what children at different Key Stages must be taught. These are called **Programmes of Study**, sometimes shortened to PoS. Each Key Stage PoS is described under different sub-headings, depending upon the subject.

Attainment Targets and Level Descriptions

As children are taught the Programmes of Study, they make different amounts of progress in learning and show variations in their understanding and abilities. The children's progress in different subjects is measured against **Attainment Targets** (ATs) which relate closely to the PoS being taught. In English, Mathematics, Science, History, Geography and Design and Technology, each AT is composed of 8 levels of increasing difficulty, level description one being the least demanding, level eight the most. However, these eight levels do *not* apply to Art, Music and PE (see below). There is an 'Exceptional Performance' level description beyond level eight, but this is very unlikely to be relevant for any child at primary school.

English

There are the same three PoS and associated ATs that apply to both KS1 and KS2:

PoS/AT 1: Speaking and Listening
PoS/AT 2: Reading
PoS/AT 3: Writing

The importance of English in the curriculum is underlined by a series of **general requirements** applicable at every key stage (see English document, pages 2–3). Pupils should be able to:

1) Communicate effectively in speech and writing (using standard English vocabulary and grammar).
2) Listen with understanding.
3) Read in an enthusiastic, responsive and well-informed way, such that they can analyse and interpret a wide range of texts.

The **Programmes of Study** for Speaking and Listening, Reading and Writing are each sub-divided into three sections:

- The *range* of opportunities that all pupils should experience.
- The *key skills* that should be taught.
- The *standard English and language study* that should characterise the teaching and learning.

English receives a lot of attention in the documentation because it permeates and touches virtually every other area of learning.

Mathematics

There are three PoS for KS1 and an additional one for KS2. Thus:

KS1 PoS:

1) Using and Applying Mathematics;
2) Number;
3) Shape, Space and Measures.

KS2 PoS:

1) Using and Applying Mathematics;
2) Number;
3) Shape, Space and Measures; *plus*
4) Handling Data.

The Attainment Targets use the same headings as the PoS except that Number and Algebra are linked under AT2. Thus:

AT1: Using and Applying Mathematics
AT2: Number and Algebra
AT3: Shape, Space and Measures
AT4: Handling Data (not applicable to KS1)

The introductions to each Key Stage (see Mathematics document, pages 2 and 6) state that stress must be placed upon the *language* of Mathematics and developing *reasoning* across the whole of work in Maths. At KS1, sorting, classifying, making comparisons and searching for patterns should apply to work on number, shape and space, and handling data. Work on measures and handling data must incorporate a knowledge of number. At KS2, measurement must be linked with handling data and with shape and space. Calculating skills must be developed in number and through work on measures and handling data. Algebraic ideas of pattern and relationships must permeate every area of Maths for older primary children.

Science

In the teaching of Science, there are general requirements which apply across all PoS (see Science document, pages 2 and 14):

- **Systematic enquiry**
- **Science in everyday life**
- **The nature of scientific ideas**
- **Communication**
- **Health and Safety**

There are four PoS and associated ATs; the same headings are used for KS1 and for KS2:

1) Experimental and Investigative Science;
2) Life Processes and Living Things;
3) Materials and their Properties;
4) Physical Processes.

Geography

The PoS for KS1 involve three areas of study:

- **Geographical Skills**
- **Places**
- **Thematic Study (a single locality at KS1; four themes at KS2).**

At KS1, pupils should be given opportunities to 'investigate the physical and human features of their surroundings, undertake studies that focus on geographical questions . . . and become aware that the world extends beyond their own locality . . .' (page 2). At KS2, pupils should have the opportunity to 'investigate places and themes across a widening range of scales, undertake studies that focus on geographical questions, develop the ability to recognise patterns . . . become aware of how places fit into a wider geographical context' (page 4).

There is a single Attainment Target in Geography.

History

History at KS1 focuses on giving pupils opportunities to develop an awareness of the past within a chronological framework. At KS2, pupils must be 'taught about important episodes and developments in Britain's past, develop a chronological framework [and] . . . investigate local history' (page 4). The whole of the History curriculum should be concerned with finding, evaluating and using evidence. There is a single Attainment Target for KS1 and for KS2, though the PoS in History are more complex than for most other subjects, especially at KS2:

KS1 PoS
Areas of Study and Key Elements to be taught together.

KS2 PoS
Study Units (six in all to be studied) and Key Elements to be taught together.

Design and Technology (D&T)

There is a single PoS for KS1 and KS2 in which Designing and Making skills (AT1) are combined with Knowledge and Understanding (AT2). Pupils must be encouraged to develop their own ideas through assignments and practical tasks, working with a range of different materials, and applying their understanding of other subject areas, notably Art, Mathematics and Science.

Art (incorporating Art, Craft and Design)

The PoS includes a basic curriculum in which all pupils should be given opportunities to experience different approaches to Art, Craft and Design as individuals and members of a group. They should develop visual perception and be taught creative, imaginative and practical skills. Significant cultural work should be studied to promote an understanding of how ideas, feelings and meanings are communicated. Lessons about visual and tactile elements of Art must be given, with due regard to health and safety, and the correct use of tools and materials. There are two Attainment Targets at both KS1 and KS2:

AT1
Investigating and Making.

AT2
Knowledge and Understanding.

Music

Music at KS1 and 2 should provide pupils with opportunities to use sounds, respond to music and make use of IT to record sounds (see page 2). They should be taught to concentrate in their listening and explore different musical elements. The musical repertoire must cover a variety of styles to allow for an appreciation of the cultural heritage. The PoS for both Key Stages is composed of two main areas to be used in conjunction, and associated two Attainment Targets:

PoS/AT1
Performing and Composing.

PoS/AT2
Listening and Appraising.

Physical Education (PE)

In Physical Education, a healthy lifestyle, positive attitudes and safe practice are integral to the teaching programme (see page 2). The PoS contain general requirements specific to each Key Stage under the major heading of Areas of Activity:

KS1
Areas of Activity: Games, Gymnastic Activities, Dance.

KS2
Areas of Activity *also* include Athletic Activities, Outdoor and Adventurous Activities, Swimming.

There is a single Attainment Target for PE.

DID YOU KNOW?
That all children should be able to swim at least 25 metres unaided, competently and safely before they leave primary school?

Assessment through Level Descriptions

Each Attainment Target has an associated set of eight **Level Descriptions** which are used by the teacher to monitor children's progress and **assess** them at the end of a Key Stage (end of Year 2 for KS1 and end of Year 6 for KS2). Teachers have to decide which level description is the best fit for each child at the end of a Key Stage.

By the end of *Key Stage 1*, the performance of the majority of children will match closely with Level Descriptions 1, 2 or 3.

By the end of *Key Stage 2*, the range will normally lie within Level Descriptions 2, 3, 4 or 5.

Some less able children may not have reached the first level, in which case they are described as **working towards Level One**. Some of these children at KS2 are likely to be diagnosed as having Special Educational Needs (SEN), requiring additional resources, such as help from a classroom assistant or specialist teaching within the mainstream school.

CASE STUDY

▼▼▼▼▼▼▼▼▼▼▼▼▼▼▼▼ ▼▼▼▼▼▼▼▼▼▼▼▼▼▼

Using Level Descriptions in Science

There are four Attainment Targets for Science; each one has eight level descriptions relating to the PoS. Thus, for Attainment Target 1 (Experimental and Investigative Science), the level descriptions contain the following phrases:

Level 1: 'Pupils describe simple features of objects . . .'

Level 2: 'Pupils respond to suggestions of how to find things out . . .'

Level 3: 'Pupils respond to suggestions, put forward their own ideas . . .'

Level 4: 'Pupils recognise the need for fair tests . . .'

Level 5: 'Pupils identify the key factors they need to consider . . .'

Level 6: 'Pupils use scientific knowledge and understanding to identify the key factors they need to consider . . .'

Level 7: Pupils use scientific knowledge and understanding to identify the key factors in situations involving a range of factors and, where appropriate, to make predictions . . .'

Level 8: 'Pupils recognise that tasks of different kinds require different strategies . . .' (DfE, 1995, *Science in the National Curriculum*)

▲▲▲▲▲▲▲▲▲▲▲▲▲▲▲▲▲▲▲▲▲▲▲▲▲▲▲▲▲▲▲▲▲▲▲▲

These extracts show that there is a progression of expectation about children's thinking and ability to contribute their own ideas as they develop their understanding of Science. By the end of Year 2, most infants will be responding to suggestions and contributing their own ideas; a few may be grasping the notion of a fair test; a few will still be limited to describing objects. By the end of Year 6, some children will still be struggling to understand concepts such as fair testing, but the majority will be identifying key factors and using their scientific knowledge constructively.

It is important to realise that there is a spread of understanding in almost every class which has to be catered for when planning lessons. Your awareness of the spread of pupils' ability will alert you to the dangers of assuming that all the children in your group or class are at comparable stages of intellectual development. It is worth looking through the level descriptions and considering their significance for your pupils. The process of matching children's attainment with level descriptions is a difficult one for teachers to manage

NOTE: It is important to distinguish between the teacher's assessment using level descriptions and the national tests in the core subjects which also take place at the end of key stages. The national tests, Standard Assessment Tasks or SATs, must be administered to all children under suitable test conditions.

and requires a lot of time and professional expertise. Although it is unlikely that you will be involved in end of Key Stage assessment, you should be aware of the content of level descriptions when you plan your lessons as they can give helpful ideas about what overall progress might be expected from most children in the class.

Art, Music and Physical Education

Art, Music and PE are not allocated level descriptions across eight levels like the other National Curriculum subjects. Instead, they have END OF KEY STAGE DESCRIPTIONS of the type and range of performance that the majority of pupils should characteristically demonstrate by the end of a Key Stage, having been taught the relevant Programmes of Study.

For instance, **Music** has two ATs ('Performing and Composing'; 'Listening and Appraising') at both KS1 and KS2, with accompanying end of key stage descriptions. The KS1 description for each Attainment Target is roughly equivalent to Level 2; the KS2 descriptions are broadly equivalent to Level 4. So, in *Music* for AT1 (Performing and Composing) we find the following expectations of children by the end of KS1:

> Pupils sing a variety of songs and play simple pieces and accompaniments with confidence . . . explore, select and order sounds, making compositions that have a simple structure . . . make expressive use of some of the musical instruments . . .

Whereas by the end of KS2:

> Pupils perform accurately and confidently . . . expressive use of the musical elements . . . awareness of phrase . . . sing songs and rounds that have two parts . . . maintain independent instrumental lines . . . select and combine resources . . . achieve a planned effect . . . use symbols when performing and communicating musical ideas. (DfE, 1995, *Music in the National Curriculum*)

A comparison of these two descriptions allows you to see the extent of progress that most children should make between the ends of the two Key Stages. It is surprisingly easy to misjudge children's capabilities and, as a result, you are likely to have inappropriate expectations of what they can achieve.

Similarly, **PE** has a description for the one Attainment Target at KS1 and the one at KS2; again, the KS1 description is approximately equivalent to Level 2; the KS2 description to Level 4. So a comparison of the descriptions for a typical child at the end of KS1 and KS2 reveals that by the end of KS1:

> Pupils plan and perform simple skills safely . . . show control in linking actions . . . improve their performance through practising their skills . . . talk about what they and others have done . . . make simple judgements . . . recognise and describe the changes that happen to their bodies during exercise.'

Whereas by the end of KS2:

> Pupils find solutions . . . practise, improve and refine performance . . . repeat series of

movements . . . with increasing control and accuracy . . . make simple judgements . . . use this information effectively . . . sustain energetic activity over appropriate periods of time . . . understand what is happening to their bodies during exercise.' (DfE, 1995, *Physical Education in the National Curriculum*)

Remember that in PE there are twice the number of Areas of Activity in KS2 relative to KS1.

Art has two ATs ('Investigating and Making'; 'Knowledge and Understanding'); once again, the descriptions for KS1 and KS2 are broadly equivalent to Level 2 and Level 4. Thus, a comparison between the end of Key Stage descriptions for KS1 and KS2 in AT2 (Knowledge and Understanding) indicates the typical pattern of development. For most children at the end of KS1:

> Pupils describe and compare images and artefacts in simple terms . . . recognise differences in methods and approaches used . . . make links with their own art, craft and design work.

Whereas by the end of KS2:

> Pupils compare images and artefacts using an art, craft and design vocabulary . . . identify similarities and differences in methods and approaches . . . begin to understand how works of art, craft and design are affected by their purpose . . . evaluate their own and others' work . . . (DfE, 1995 *Art in the National Curriculum*)

REMINDER: The eight end of Key Stage Levels of Attainment do not apply to Art, Music and PE. National tests only apply to the three core subjects: Maths, English, and Science.

End of key stage descriptions are needed for Art, Music and PE for three main reasons:

- **it gives teachers something to use as a guide in evaluating how their pupils are progressing;**
- **it informs curriculum planning;**
- **it is useful for communicating children's progress to their parents.**

Are you confused?

If so, don't be too upset. Qualified teachers find that they need to work with the curriculum regularly before they become comfortable with the details. Nevertheless, it pays to persevere with your mastery of the National Curriculum content and procedures. If you are in the early stages of your training, knowledge of the core subjects and your own specialist subject should be your priority.

TEST YOURSELF

How well have you absorbed the details about the National Curriculum? To find out, try the following set of questions. The answers to them can be found in the middle of page 50.

1) Name the three Core Subjects of the National Curriculum.
2) How many Foundation Subjects are there?
3) What other subject forms part of the curriculum?
4) Name the six subjects which contain eight level descriptions.
5) Which additional sub-area is found for Mathematics KS2 compared with KS1?
6) How many Attainment Targets are there for Design and Technology?
7) What are the three Attainment Target headings for KS1 and KS2 English?
8) What is specifically demanded for the two PoS sub-areas in History at KS1 and KS2?
9) How many themes have to be studied in Geography at KS2?
10) What are the two Attainment Targets for Art?
11) Which three subjects have end-of-key-stage descriptions rather than level descriptions?
12) What description is given to children who have not reached Level 1 in the core subjects?

Answers

1) Mathematics, English, Science.
2) Six.
3) Religious Education, RE.
4) Maths, English, Science, History, Geography, Design & Technology.
5) Handling data.
6) Two.
7) Speaking and Listening, Reading, Writing.
8) That they are studied in conjunction.
9) Four.
10) Investigating and Making; Knowledge and Understanding.
11) Art, Music, PE.
12) Working towards level 1.

NATIONAL CURRICULUM SUMMARY

The three **Core** subjects: Mathematics, English, Science.
The six **Foundation** subjects: Design and Technology, History, Geography, Art, Music, Physical Education.
The **tenth** subject: Religious Education.
Information Technology should be used across the curriculum.

Programmes of Study: the content specified for each curriculum subject.
Attainment Targets: descriptions of progress arranged under eight levels (level descriptions) for the core subjects and end of key stage descriptions for the foundation subjects.

Most children in core subjects are expected to have attained levels 1, 2 or 3 by the end of KS1, and levels 2, 3, 4 and 5 by the end of KS2.

There are **statutory tests** (SATs) at the end of each Key Stage in the core subjects for every child. Teachers also provide their own assessments based on their knowledge of the children by using the level descriptions for different Attainment Targets.

The place of Information Technology

Information Technology is most commonly seen in schools through the use of computers. Computers are intended to be used for learning across the curriculum, primarily as a support for different subjects, but also as a way of becoming familiar with the machine's use and function.

Calculators in school

Children have to be familiar with calculators as a learning tool for computation across different areas of the curriculum. Calculators must be used in conjunction with the mastery of number bonds (checking answers, for instance), and not as a substitute for mental arithmetic. The over-reliance of children on calculators has led to many schools designing a structured learning programme specifically to control their use.

Finally

The National Curriculum and testing is intended to support your teaching rather than suffocate it. Familiarity with its content and assessment will enhance your classroom practice if you use the information purposefully. However, the imagination and enterprise with which you plan and carry out your lessons is a function of many other factors, explored in the following chapters.

CHAPTER 5

Lesson Preparation

Planning for learning is about setting aims and objectives, converting them into teaching intentions and then allowing the children, through various activities, to translate them into a whole spectrum of knowledge, skills and understandings appropriate to them

(Moyles, 1992)

Teachers have to be competent in many areas, including personal relationships, organisation of teaching and learning, time management, evaluation of pupil's progress, working as a member of a team, reporting to parents and contributing subject expertise to a whole staff effort. However, without effective lesson preparation and high quality teaching learning will be a drudgery, and children will never make the progress of which they are capable. Lessons provide the forum in which your teaching skills can be applied in such a way that learning becomes a rich and meaningful experience for your pupils.

THE TEACHING FILE

One of the practical ways in which you can increase your chances of success in teaching is through ensuring that documentation is kept orderly and accessible. It is wishful thinking to believe that you can prosper as a teacher simply by gathering together a few ideas about what you will teach without careful consideration about how you will go about it. Random ideas applied to classroom situations will wither in the heat of the daily need for continuity of learning.

Ideas are important, but they need to be woven into a consistent and structured approach if they are to help children learn. To assist in structuring the teaching and learning process, your college will probably provide you with guidelines for maintaining a **school experience file**. The file, often contained within a ring-binder, is used to contain all of the documents, plans and records required for your time in school. Files require effort to maintain, and a good one should fulfil two main purposes:

- **it should support your teaching by containing lesson plans and supporting documentation such as records of children's progress and examples of their written work.**
- **it should demonstrate to your supervisor that you are developing a healthy critical awareness of your role as a teacher through the inclusion of descriptions of events, analyses of the learning process and reflections upon ways to improve your teaching.**

Although the detailed contents of the file will depend upon your college guidelines, school circumstances and your own preference for organising, it is essential that the file is *usable*. You may produce a meticulously maintained file, but if it is inaccessible or of little help in your teaching, it is hardly worth bothering to keep it. Always ensure that the opening page contains essential information such as the name of the school, your own name, and the names of the class teacher and the supervisor. The remainder of the file should be sub-divided with headings at the start of each section and include:

- *Basic Information*: **class lists, group lists, dinner arrangements, timetables, maps of the school, names of significant people (head teacher, class teacher, and so on)**
- *The School's Curriculum Programme*: **patterns of teaching across the year, strategies for assessment in the core subjects**
- *Preliminary planning and plans*: **all the lesson plans and planning ideas that you have developed before commencing your teaching experience**
- *Lesson plans*: **details of individual lessons for each day planned throughout your time in school. The plans can be arranged consecutively in a chronology, lesson by lesson, as they are taught throughout the week, or by clustering subjects/areas together. For instance, all the maths lessons could be placed together, all the geography lessons, all the thematic or topic lessons, and so on.**
- *Evaluations*: **sometimes referred to as** *lesson reviews*. **Written reflections upon your progress are normally required by the college. You can keep the reviews adjacent to the lessons to which they apply or in a separate section specifically for the purpose. If you choose to keep them with the individual lessons, it is useful to write the comments on different coloured paper to distinguish them from lesson plans. With the development of Career Entry Profiles (CEPs), your evaluations should be supported by specific** *evidence* **from your teaching to support your claims about the quality of your teaching (see Chapter 8).**
- *Assessments and records*: **information about children's progress and achievements should be placed in this section. For instance, reading records, spelling test results, evidence of children's achievements and photographs of work can be included. Bear in mind that other forms of evidence about progress are less easy to identify. Thus, classroom ethos, collaborative investigations and large space lessons like PE, though part of the learning process, are difficult to assess and record.**
- *Master copies*: **examples of worksheets, activity sheets, good ideas, proformas, tips for good practice, schedules**

The school experience file is not meant to be an end in itself, but to service your teaching and help you to keep the complexities of teaching in good order. Although a well maintained file does not guarantee success, it is often a sign of a potentially good teacher. Some colleges suggest that you keep a general teaching file AND a separate file of evidence. This is called the Professional Development Portfolio (PDP) and informs the CEP.

DIRECTED TASKS

Some teaching experiences are for the purpose of carrying out specific tasks and activities agreed between the college and the school. For instance, you may be asked to make a game to use in Maths or English, hear four children read, teach three lessons on a particular topic or assess the progress made by five children in core subjects. These tasks may be linked with an assignment; you may be asked to reflect upon your teaching success; a partner may observe you and offer subsequent feedback. It is important to treat these responsibilities seriously and document them carefully.

PLANS AND PLANNING

Planning is the process of thinking, consultation and developing ideas that leads to the production of plans which act as a guide for your lessons. The planning process is continuous, as insights gained through using plans in teaching result in further planning. More effective plans can then be written that more accurately reflect the children's learning needs. Plans and planning are at the heart of effective teaching and learning, so before you begin your teaching experience, you need to spend a lot of time thinking about what you want children to learn and how you intend to go about it. There are three stages of planning in the production of plans.

Stage 1

Find out from the class teacher as much as you can about:

- *Whether there are any schemes of work of which you need to be aware.*
The school staff will already have a list of broad topic headings or subject areas expressed through their agreed plans, especially for the foundation subjects. Most schools have a continuous scheme of work for Maths, sometimes dependent upon a text book or series of work cards for each specific area.
- *The on-going work in the core subjects.*
Schools place great emphasis upon the teaching of English. For instance, as part of their language acquistion programme, younger children will often be taught phonics (recognising and correctly pronouncing letter sounds) as discrete lessons. Similarly, junior or children aged 7 to 11 years will almost certainly have regular lessons which focus on aspects of grammar (such as sentence construction). Some schools combine elements of core subjects into the current topic or theme. For instance, a topic about 'People we meet' for children in Year 1 might be

based principally upon aspects of Geography and RE, but almost certainly incorporate aspects of English (such as reading about different family groups or writing letters to a local Community leader) and Maths (such as graphs showing people's preferences). Similarly, a History study unit (such as 'Life in Tudor times') will, in addition to an understanding of the significance of the events of that period, involve discussion about the nature of historical evidence, scrutiny of documentation and written accounts of key events.

- *What the children have already covered.*

It is very disheartening for you to spend hours of work preparing a lesson that turns out to be unsuitable because the children have passed that point in their learning. You need to find out what children know and understand, the skills they possess, and their awareness of how different parts of their learning fit together, before planning future lessons. The class teacher will supply you with some details, but you will gain further insights through talking with the children and looking at their work.

In these ways, you should gain a clear picture of the school's approach to organising learning and the class teacher's particular priorities with that age group. One reason for spending time with the class teacher before the formal start of your school placement is that she can provide you with vital information about the children's progress and past experience.

If you are teaching very young children, it is likely that the *timetable* will consist of the specific times that the class uses the hall for PE, swimming times, any lessons that require specialist equipment or expertise (such as Music) and regular sessions during the day for story, group discussions or television viewing. Older pupils may have a more specific timetable of lessons, particularly in Maths, English and Science. Specialist teachers are sometimes used for Design and Technology, Music, Games and (if appropriate) first language tuition or a modern foreign language.

Stage 2

Agree with your supervisor and class teacher how much you will be expected to teach during the first two weeks or so of the placement. It is important to be as precise as possible, but beware of giving the impression that you are the sort of student who works to rule or is inflexible. It is normal for students to increase their responsibilities gradually as the weeks pass, so avoid taking on too much teaching too soon. On the other hand, do not keep putting off the time when you extend your range of responsibilities or you could limit your development as a teacher. In the early stages of a teaching experience, you may find that you only have to teach single lessons in isolation, such as taking a single group for maths or a whole class story at the end of a morning. Gradually, you will plan lessons across several weeks to ensure continuity of teaching and learning.

Stage 3

Look carefully at the appropriate National Curriculum Programmes of Study (PoS). The school plans will certainly make reference to the PoS in their own planning documentation, so it should be easy for you to find the appropriate document and plan your lesson with that information in mind. Remember that the PoS are for guidance; they provide a framework rather than a blueprint for lesson planning. Once you have the PoS clearly in your mind, and accessible in your file, you will only need to refer to them occasionally.

Your teaching is significant for the children, but should not be isolated from the other parts of their learning gained in previous years, at school and at home. If you are teaching new entrants (aged four or five years), information from a baseline assessment will help you to gain a fuller picture of individual children's experience and potential. Your planning will be helped if you can take a step back from the immediacy of preparing single lessons and see your teaching as part of a much bigger educational enterprise. Baseline assessments of children provide teachers with a picture of their existing knowledge, understanding and skills. In the case of very young children, their social skills are also included. Baseline assessments are helpful in the case of children who change school, those who are beginning a new phase in their education (such as entering a different Key Stage) and beginners. Information for beginners is normally provided by parents, though schools also carry out their own assessments. For children at other stages of their school career, information is normally provided by the previous school or teacher.

DIFFERENT TYPES OF PLANS

All schools have a developmental programme in which the different areas of the National Curriculum are set out in broad terms over a period of two or more years to ensure that the children will receive their full curriculum entitlement over a key stage. These long-term plans are sometimes referred to as a *rolling programme* to indicate a pattern of curriculum provision which ensures that the same content is not repeated from year to year. The children's understanding is also built up through reinforcing their knowledge and skills at different points as they move through the school. In this way, children reconstruct their understanding and gain deeper insights and expertise. The school's curriculum plans may be displayed on the staffroom wall.

The school will already have broad headings for curriculum coverage during each year, often based around half-termly plans. So if the school's plans specify that a particular half-term will be spent on a Geography theme such as 'Types of settlement', there is little point in expecting to teach a theme about 'World climate'. In most schools, these topic headings do not incorporate Mathematics, which is largely taught independently from other subject areas. It is essential that you find out as much as you can about curriculum plans for the detailed block of time coinciding with the period of your teaching experience:

- the *curriculum content* for each subject or topic;
- the *patterns of learning* for the children according to their needs and experience.

The curriculum content provides a close description of what has to be covered, and may make reference to particular approaches and ideas for the development of children's understanding. For instance, the use of computer Maths games may be a central component of learning in 'Shape, space and measures'. Again, a visit to a local field centre may be a required part of 'Geographical skills'.

The patterns of learning refer to organisation of classes, grouping of children, broad assessment of progress and monitoring of standards. For instance, a group of teachers may combine their classes for certain lessons and teach together, each being responsible for a specific element of the subject or topic. Over a period of weeks, both groups are taught by each teacher, ensuring that all the children in every class receive the benefit of teacher expertise.

Lessons plans

While the school's existing half-termly plans are an important guide in your preparation for teaching experience, they lack the detail required for individual lessons. You need to develop your individual lesson plans within the framework of the school's plans, guided by teachers, tutors or anyone who can offer support. Some class teachers are happy to give advice about lesson ideas; others feel that students should be more self-sufficient and develop their own. In practice, the best lesson plans draw upon a combination of tried-and-tested approaches suggested by experienced practitioners and your own creative ideas.

At the start of a FASE, you are normally only asked to teach a small number of lessons to a small group of children (perhaps four or five children per group). Even this prospect can seem quite daunting when you are new to the school and feeling tense. Although this unease fades after a week or so, many students still get anxious about what to *do* in lessons, let alone how to teach effectively! Two things are worth remembering:

- *Lesson preparation is made easier if you realise that it forms only a part of the overall sequence of learning.*
  The expression *individual* lesson is not always helpful, for learning is rarely done in a single lesson. If your lesson can be prepared with an eye to previous ones, and with a reasonably clear view of what is to follow, it has a better chance of succeeding.
- *What you do affects how you do it.*
  A lesson idea must always be considered in conjunction with the way you organise the learning. For instance, a lesson which requires active co-operation by groups of children is much harder to arrange than one in which everyone works individually on the same task.

Sequencing of lessons is an important part of short-term planning. Lessons need to show continuity or they become fragmented and children lose track of what is happening. This does not mean that the pattern of each session has to be identical. For instance, you might prepare three consecutive Maths lessons on aspects of shape, followed by one session applying the ideas in a problem-solving exercise. If the three lessons and problem-solving session together have a single overall purpose and are mutually dependent, you have produced a valid short-term plan in Mathematics (see Figure 5.1 on page 58). In reality, most of your planning will be of this sequencing type, involving a chain of lessons rather than solitary ones.

Sometimes, short-term plans involve more than one curriculum area. For instance, if

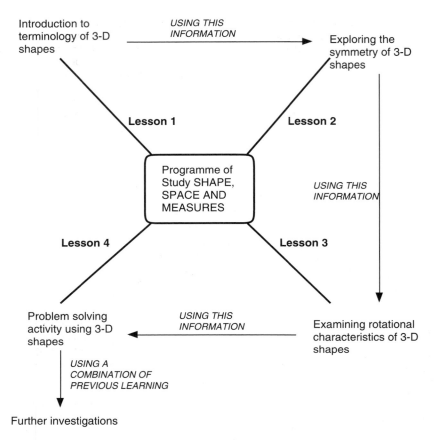

Figure 5.1 Short-term plan

you are teaching children about designing a new town centre as a contribution towards a local debate over pedestrianisation, your series of lessons within the short-term plan might cover a fortnight of work, and include aspects of Geography, Mathematics, Design and Technology, and Information Technology. An important component of your lessons might involve children examining maps of the area, reading accounts in the local newspaper, writing letters to counsellors, designing alternative road systems and estimating the likely costs of the project. These letters and plans might necessitate the use of computers and graphic design programs. Although the skills associated with examining maps, designing and estimating and so on might also be considered during separate lessons on other occasions, they would all be relevant to work on the project (see Figure 5.2 on page 59).

Whether for a solitary lesson or one which forms part of a series, your plans should show the following three aspects for each subject or area of learning:

- ■ *The learning experiences the children have already had.*
  Find out initially by asking the teacher and the children. Eventually, you won't need to ask anyone as *you* will have taught the previous lesson.

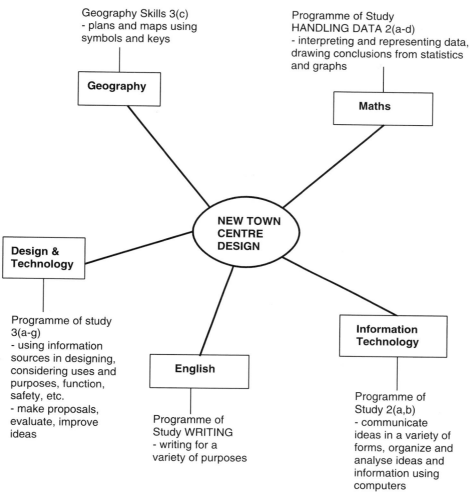

Geography Skills 3(c)
- plans and maps using symbols and keys

Geography

Programme of Study
HANDLING DATA 2(a-d)
- interpreting and representing data, drawing conclusions from statistics and graphs

Maths

NEW TOWN CENTRE DESIGN

Design & Technology

Programme of study 3(a-g)
- using information sources in designing, considering uses and purposes, function, safety, etc.
- make proposals, evaluate, improve ideas

English

Programme of Study WRITING
- writing for a variety of purposes

Information Technology

Programme of Study 2(a,b)
- communicate ideas in a variety of forms, organize and analyse ideas and information using computers

Figure 5.2 New Town Centre Design – Key Stage 2

- ■ *The main purpose of your present lesson.*
Use documentation, either directly from National Curriculum booklets or ideas gained from elsewhere.
- ■ *The likely future direction of lessons.*
'Where next?' should always form part of your thinking about the present lesson.

For instance, a poetry lesson might take account of the following factors:

The children's previous learning experiences
Work on humorous rhymes and non-rhyming couplets in pairs to produce short poems about everyday sounds. Links with drama (acting out the poems in small groups).

Present lesson
Use of tape containing unusual sounds; development of appropriate vocabulary; written examples of published poems on the subject; collaborative group work to produce a group poem.

Likely future experience

Enlarging vocabulary through the introduction of more complex poems, expressing written ideas through choral speaking; developing poems for presentation to some younger children, utilising percussion instruments to create accompanying sound effects.

Although the present lesson will require a more thorough and detailed description, this will be simpler once your thinking is clear about the lesson's place in a child's overall experience. It also helps you to be able to show children that you are aware of their previous learning, explain where the present lesson fits in, and enthuse them by hinting at the exciting things that lie ahead. In this respect, *clarity of purpose* is essential (see Figure 5.3 below).

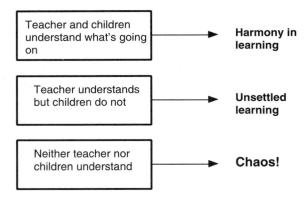

Figure 5.3 Clarity of purpose in learning

Single lesson plans

You may be less interested in sequences of lessons and more concerned about surviving a couple of individual ones. This is an understandable attitude if you are new to the classroom. If you are inexperienced or in the first week or so of your school experience, you may find that preparation of individual lessons is as much as you can cope with. As we have noted, when you relax and gain confidence, you will normally pay more attention to sequences of lessons than to single ones. Over the period of a placement, the individual lesson plans merge into a more coherent set of teaching-and-learning experiences that take account of children's abilities, time factors and the effectiveness of different teaching techniques.

The format for your lesson plans will vary slightly according to the age-group of children and the curriculum focus, but all plans should pay attention to certain key elements shown below.

THE LESSON'S PURPOSE OR INTENTION

Some students have a good idea for a lesson but spend little time considering its purpose and how they will know if the purpose has been realised. The purpose may relate to a new skill that the children have to master, practising a known skill, enlarging understanding, working collaboratively on solving a problem, or a combination of these. Your lesson purpose should ideally be linked with National Curriculum documentation or the school's policy, and contain a reference to the Programmes of Study. However, bear in mind that lessons are not always predictable and unexpected opportunities can arise for learning. Although a lesson purpose is an essential guide to your planning, it is not to be compared with a ten-pin bowling alley with the lesson objectives waiting like pins to be bowled over by your brilliant teaching! The complexity of the learning process means that the ball sometimes has a mind of its own and moves off in a slightly different direction – or flies completely off course.

THE PROBABLE SEQUENCE OF EVENTS

Every lesson follows some sequence, either by design or default. Students who give careful thought to the lesson's likely pattern (introduction, distribution of resources, settling, time-on-task, conclusion and so on) in the early part of their teaching normally discover that it becomes less necessary to be as precise as the weeks go by. If you are very inexperienced, it pays to write down some approximate timings alongside the different parts of the lesson: introduction 3 minutes; question-and-answer 5 minutes . . . and so on. Although this precision can be counter-productive if it restricts your flexibility in teaching, it is worth practising your lesson with a sympathetic friend beforehand to gain a feel for the time it takes before trying it out.

RESOURCES

Almost all students have found to their anguish that they have given insufficient attention to resourcing. Paper is uncut, felt pens run dry, books are unexpectedly missing from the library, too many children try to share too few pieces of equipment and so on. Each lesson plan should not only indicate the resources required but, in the early stages of a teaching experience, give specific information about their whereabouts and accessibility. As far as possible, train children to take responsibility for gathering their own basic resources. But one way or another, do not leave anything to chance.

DIFFERENTIATION (MATCHING)

Even a group of children who are supposedly of the same academic level contains a spread of ability and enthusiasm. Although it is difficult to make allowance for the variety of children's needs in a class, you should at least indicate in your lesson notes how you have tried to take account of them. In most classes, children are set tasks on the basis of their ability. However, this does not take account of the speed at which they work and their application to the task. You need to allow for the fact that some children work fast and carelessly, others slow and accurately. Slow workers are not necessarily less able, but may find difficulty in applying themselves. Your lesson plan should normally include an open-ended element for genuinely faster and more capable children who otherwise might become bored and restless with nothing to do. The open-ended element can include a list of things to find out, a challenge to make up a problem for a friend, a library search, or anything which will self sufficiently stretch their minds.

ASSESSMENT OF WORK AND FEEDBACK

Although it is difficult for you to give children immediate and detailed feedback during, or at the end of every session (or lesson), it is easier if you have clarified your expectations in your lesson plan. If you do not know what you expect from the children, it is difficult for you to monitor what they do, praise their endeavours, help them to do better, or gauge the success of the teaching session. In doing this, you need to have some idea of the school's policy for marking work. Do children receive a star, a mark out of ten, a grade, a written comment, or what? How will you assess the quality of their non-written work such as drawings, artwork, drama or clay models? It is normal to offer constructive verbal *feedback* to assist the children in developing their skills or understanding during a single lesson (**formative assessment**). You will certainly want to evaluate their progress during the lesson (**evaluative assessment**). However, at the end of a lesson or several lessons, you may make an assessment which summarises what they have achieved (**summative assessment**) through a written test or formal questions-and-answers. The sensitivity with which you handle aspects of assessment makes a huge difference to pupils' motivation and confidence. Reference to your strategy for assessment of children's work should be based firmly on the class teacher's approach, and included in a prominent place in your file.

LINKS WITH OTHER LESSONS

Lessons in the very early stages of teaching tend to be self-contained while you become familiar with the pace and atmosphere of classroom life. However, as you gain confidence, your lessons should be *sequenced* so that the children's learning is more continuous. Every lesson plan should have a sub-heading at the bottom of the page, entitled 'where next?'. Figure 5.4 below shows a lesson outline appropriate to teaching the core subjects.

Intention: Things children should learn from this lesson.

National Curriculum links: The appropriate Programme of Study documentation provided for the subject.

Knowledge base: Things children need to know already in order to understand the current lesson.

Vocabulary: Key terms to introduce, develop or extend the children's understanding.

Questions: A list of questions to ask the children to ascertain how much they already know.

Engagement: The way in which, early on in the lesson, children will be convinced that the lesson is going to be interesting.

Introduction: Telling the children what they are going to be doing, how it will happen and what is expected from them.

Main course: The core of the lesson . . . what the teacher will say; how much activity the children will do; occasions when the teacher stands back to allow children to explore and investigate; how much the teacher intervenes and offers guidance; how long the main course lasts; how it will conclude.

Sunset: The final stage of the lesson . . . anticipated outcomes; storage of work; time for evaluating the lesson with the children; opportunity for the children to comment; clearing up; leaving things straight.

Extension and early finisher activities: For children who complete the activity unexpectedly quickly. Where next?

Figure 5.4 Lesson plan for core subjects

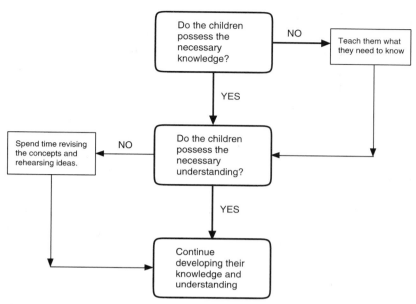

Figure 5.5 Reviewing existing knowledge and understanding

Making links

Earlier sections have already underlined the importance of making links with the children's previous learning experiences. During the first few minutes of a lesson, you should always spend a little time *recapping* relevant earlier lessons, asking appropriate questions to ascertain the children's knowledge and understanding, and correcting any misconceptions (see Figure 5.5).

Take care over the way that you express yourself. For instance, avoid saying: 'You remember what I said last time about . . .'. There is a good chance that at least one person will call out that they do not remember. You are then placed in a position in which you either have to ignore what is said (when the child was being honest) or enter a dialogue with the child, running the risk that others in the class will begin to talk among themselves while you do so. Furthermore, you are faced with the task of calling the class to order and re-establishing your control before the lesson can continue. It is better to say: 'Last time I gave you three examples of . . .' and summarise the main points clearly; or 'Put your hand up if you remember . . .' and point to individuals for a response.

If you select to *ask questions* rather than inform the children, it is important to listen carefully to children's answers and not allow interruptions from others while an individual child is struggling to express ideas. Extending your arm with your palm facing outwards (like someone stopping traffic) while you listen intently to another child's response will act as a deterrent to anyone who tends to call out.

If you decide to summarise the previous lesson through *informing* them of the main points, it may be useful to use a *visual aid* to remind the class of the most significant points:

1) by writing the key points on the board;
2) by use of a large sheet on which you have already listed the points in dark, readable felt pen;

3) by using *two* overhead projector transparencies: the first with the *key* points to summarise the previous lesson, the second with the *additional* points relating to the present lesson that can be superimposed upon the first sheet to give the children a fuller picture of the lesson's direction.

The disadvantage with option 1) is that your back is turned to the class while you write, thereby losing eye contact and risking inattentive behaviour. Your handwriting must also be clear and large enough for everyone to see.

Option 2) is best done in advance of the lesson. It is essential that everyone can see the words clearly and that you don't have to walk around the room carrying the sheet like a billboard.

Option 3), using OHP transparencies, is an excellent method, providing they are carefully prepared and visually stimulating. There may also be a logistical problem with siting the projector (see pages 103–104).

Whatever method you use to recap earlier ideas, there are two points to consider:

- **some children may not have been present during the previous lesson;**
- **some children may have forgotten or failed to understand what you said last time.**

If a child informs you that she was *absent* during the lesson, you can thank her and assure her that you will give her some extra help in due course. Do not, of course, forget your promise. If children's blank looks, lack of interest or unsatisfactory responses suggest that the previous lesson *made little impact*, you will need to have some strategies for *revising* the concepts, skills or knowledge. This revision process can be accomplished in various ways.

WHEN KNOWLEDGE OF CONTENT IS IMPORTANT

You can ask the children direct questions with a single correct answer. Your questions should be graded, using simple ones come first so that every child feels able to answer. With easier questions, try to select a child to answer who is unlikely to have an answer to the harder ones. Do not forget to praise the child who answers sincerely (if incorrectly) and commend all those who had their hand raised but were not asked. When asking more difficult questions, insist that children pause to think about their response before raising their hands. Generally, never ask for an answer from a child who is grunting and straining to answer, or you will soon have a classroom resembling a herd of hungry pigs!

WHEN UNDERSTANDING OF TECHNIQUE IS IMPORTANT

Demonstrate slowly and carefully the particular technique used in the previous lesson, explaining both what you are doing and why you are doing it. It is important to say out loud the significance of what you are doing as you proceed. This stimulates your pupils' thinking and engages their interest. Be ready to respond to children's spontaneous remarks and questions.

WHEN ACCURACY IS IMPORTANT

Read an account of (say) the relevant event or incident, making *deliberate mistakes* with key words as you do so. Do not allow yourself to be interrupted until you have finished reading. At the end, ask the children to suggest the number of mistakes you have made.

You can then repeat the reading, emphasising the key words (and giving the correct ones) as you go along. This approach can be very effective if used occasionally, but it takes thorough preparation. You have to have your own carefully annotated copy of the reading, of course. A variation on this method is to ask the children to count the mistakes silently as you proceed, then ask for them to raise their hands if they think you made more than five mistakes, more than ten . . . and so on. You can then repeat the reading, using the correct words, but using a slightly different intonation for those words to emphasise them. Discussion about the nature of the errors can be used positively as a revision strategy.

Approaches for recapping and revising earlier lessons should be included in your plans. Ideally, parts of the work that children have failed to grasp should be identified at the end of the previous lesson in the sunset stage (see Figure 5.4 on page 62) rather than at the start of the next lesson. Following the lesson, when you have had time to reflect on the children's learning and examine the work they have produced, you may identify areas of weakness or where further clarification is needed. However, by the next lesson some children will have forgotten what you thought they knew, so recapping is essential.

> **CONSIDER**
> It is said that some people who go abroad and cannot made themselves understood repeat the same phrase louder and louder in the hope that it will somehow sink in! Successful teachers, on the other hand, try different strategies rather than repeating unsuccessful methods.

It is also important to find methods for revising that are *different* from the teaching methods you used in the original lesson. If not, you may find that you waste time going over old ground in the same unsatisfactory way that prevented the pupils from learning very much in the first place.

CASE STUDY

We have seen that if you are unsure about what you are doing, it is unlikely that you will be able to explain a task adequately to the children. You must establish your lesson purpose before deciding how it is to be achieved. The lesson *purpose* (or intention) should be established first and the lesson *format* (what happens during the lesson to achieve the purpose) should follow.

For instance, imagine that you have been told to work with a group of six year-olds to investigate aspects of floating and sinking (Key Stage 1 Programme of Study, 'Experimental and Investigative Science'). Beforehand, you mention it to a friend who tells you that she has done floating and sinking with a Year 1 class before. She explains that 'all you have to do' is use a tank full of water, make sure that the children wear aprons, gather a variety of articles that float and others that sink, and let the children

NOTE: When your teaching experience begins, it is possible that you will have done a lot of planning but have relatively few actual plans in place. This is because it is difficult for even the best students to get to know their class situations well enough prior to their time in school to establish their plans firmly. Plans will become more secure during the first couple of weeks as the classroom situation becomes more familiar to you.

try each in turn for themselves. Finally, you let the children draw the objects on paper and stick them on a chart under two headings: 'Things that float'; 'Things that sink'.

The idea sounds promising, but what is the purpose of doing it? If it is to show children that some objects float and some sink, it is very limited in what it seeks to achieve. A lesson purpose must be more detailed and linked to what the children already know and understand. For instance, after ascertaining that the children know that certain objects float and sink by asking them careful questions which allow them to share their knowledge with you, or demonstrating the fact in front of them using a variety of objects, the lesson should relate to a purpose covered by one or more of the following:

- **to vary the shape of a material (tin foil, for example) to create the best shape for floating;**
- **to compare the length of time it takes certain objects to sink;**
- **to find out how much weight (number of marbles, for example) an object will hold before sinking.**

It is obvious from these few examples that a lesson might span several separate sessions as different aspects of floating and sinking are examined and discussed. You can raise questions as the children experiment and gain first-hand experiences of different materials; you can relate what is happening to familiar occurrences (such as bath toys) or wider issues of health and safety (such as the importance of buoyancy aids such as water wings). The children can represent their findings in different ways: drawings, diagrams, writing, or even a simple piece of drama. Whatever emphasis you give to the lesson, you should be clear about your intentions about what the children should learn and understand, and provide appropriate resources and activities to support that learning.

Values and teaching

The way that you approach teaching will depend in large measure upon the things you value in education. Contrast, for instance, someone who believes that children should be passive recipients of knowledge waiting for the teacher to provide it, with someone who believes that children should be active learners, ask searching questions and develop the study skills to find out for themselves. It is obvious that the teacher with the first set of principles will organise the children's learning in a very different way from the second one. For instance, the first teacher will probably tend to teach the class as a whole, emphasise individual learning and awarding marks. The second teacher is likely to organise learning in a way which depends upon collaborative problem-solving, invite children's opinions about issues and engage them in a dialogue about the work.

There are many variations and combinations of the two stereotypes described above, and teachers often use a variety of methods for different areas and subjects. A teacher may believe that a more formal arrangement is appropriate for teaching the core subjects, and a more investigative, interactive arrangement for other curriculum subjects and topics. Everything that teachers do in the classroom is underpinned by their values and beliefs about teaching and learning. Sometimes, in the earliest stages of your teaching experience, you may do things because you are imitating an experienced teacher, because you read about it in a book, or because the class teacher says that it is best. Gradually, as you gain confidence, it is essential to stop and ask yourself the searching question: 'Why am I doing things this way?'

It is important that you have some broad principles about education that you can apply to every school situation, with an idea of the implications for practical teaching. The best teachers are always modifying their teaching approach and looking for ways to enhance their effectiveness as a result. If you intend getting the most out of your FASE, you must follow their example.

THINK THE LESSON THROUGH BEFOREHAND

The habit of thinking the lesson through carefully before you embark upon it is one worth cultivating. Some students prepare a lesson while sitting at home and imagine that it can be transferred smoothly to the classroom situation without taking account of the practicalities. In this case lessons become like an item in a travelling salesman's case – produced for an audience and used regardless of the context. However, a successful lesson must take close account of the learning situation, layout of furniture, availability of resources, movement around the room and the particular children involved. Thinking the lesson through means examining *every* aspect from start to finish ...

- *Where will the children be as you approach the classroom?*
  Lined up outside; sitting in the classroom waiting; milling about ... ?
- *Where are the resources for the lesson?*
  In a cupboard; spread out on tables; in boxes ... ?
- *How will you settle the children?*
  Clapping your hands; raising your hand; sitting at your desk and staring around the room ... ?
- *How will the lesson commence?*
  By continuing with work already begun; an explanation; reviewing an earlier lesson; a series of questions; telling a story ... ?
- *What happens next?*
  The children divide into groups; work in pairs; work singly ... ?

Each part of the lesson should be rehearsed and mentally scrutinised. As you think about the realities of classroom life, it will reduce the likelihood that you will be caught out by making elementary mistakes. Although it is impossible to predict everything, **forewarned**

is forearmed. As part of increasing your awareness, consider how the classroom context might also affect your approach.

Classroom context

The classroom in which you teach sometimes affects what you are able to do. If you are restricted by space, access or lack of resources, you have little choice but to modify your lesson accordingly. For instance, some activities require water, and would be unsuitable for a busy corridor unless suitable safeguards were included. Other activities require natural light or need access to a workbench or to a spacious area. Even in a conventional classroom, large numbers of children can restrict the range and nature of practical activities due to a lack of resources or the impossibility of having too many children involved in tasks that require movement, discussion and experimentation.

NOISE LEVELS

Noise levels must also be considered. For example, any attempt at a lesson exploring percussion sounds in a room adjoining another teacher hearing children read is likely to make you rather unpopular. Similarly, a joint venture by a group of five children to act out a play in the library area when other children are using books for research would be equally unwise. The context has an influence upon what you do and how you do it, and you must take account of it when thinking things through in advance if you are to get the most out of your teaching and allow other teachers to do the same.

ROOM LAYOUT

Room layout can significantly affect the success of your lessons. Some rooms contain tables; others contain desks. Some tables can be pushed together for practical work, others cannot. Sometimes, chairs and other items of furniture block pathways and make movement difficult across the room. This does not mean that you should be timid in attempting different activities, but realistic about the practicalities of doing them. Figures 5.6 to 5.8 on pages 70 and 71 show three different classroom layouts that you may encounter in schools. Notice some of the differences between them:

Figure 5.6 on page 70 has a number of different activity areas: painting, Maths and Language, computers, sand play. There are also two book shelves, one in a prominent position close to the carpet area, one underneath a board. There is a single entrance point, resources are placed strategically around the room, and there are two small tables close to another large board. The teacher's desk is tucked away in a corner. An overhead projector (OHP) is located close to the second board. In contrast to the informal layout of activity areas, the children's tables are arranged in a fairly formal manner, each seat facing the same way. There are a number of conclusions we can reach from studying this layout:

- **the different work areas suggest that the teacher divides the class into activity groups for working;**
- **the prominence of the bookshelves indicates that children are encouraged to browse and select for themselves;**
- **the OHP suggests that the teacher teaches formally on occasions;**

■ **the orderly desk arrangement shows that the teacher does not favour collaborative activity other than in the activity areas.**

Notice, too, that the classroom door opens onto the hall. This means that nearly all activities must take place within the classroom as there is no adjacent work space outside it. In judging the appropriateness of your lesson, you have to make allowance for the constraints and opportunities presented by this classroom layout.

By contrast, Figure 5.7 on page 70 has a large floor tiled area in one corner of the room, a large carpeted area with a small board, numerous entrance and exit points, and tables in two tight groups. The computer station, work table and fiction books are all located in the wide corridor outside the main door. This classroom layout indicates that this teacher manages her classroom differently from the first teacher:

■ **the distinctive positioning of the art, craft and science resources suggests that practical subjects are organised separately from other activities;**
■ **the dispersion of work areas may necessitate additional adult support;**
■ **the table configurations indicate that seat work is collaborative rather than individual;**
■ **the location of some resources outside the main classroom suggests that children have to be trained to work unsupervised for some period of the day;**
■ **the small boards facilitate small-group teaching rather than whole class;**
■ **the swing doors suggest that there is close liaison between classes and the opportunity for team teaching and joint supervision by teachers.**

Figure 5.8 on page 71 shows another configuration. The small ante-room is available for whole class briefings or (if there is a second adult available to supervise the rest of the class) teaching a single group. The shared practical area necessitates joint planning with teachers of the other classes who use the area. The steps, open access and close proximity of tables indicate that movement of children around the area has to be carefully controlled.

The classroom in Figure 5.9 on page 71 is extremely formal. Most of the teaching will be from the front of the class to the whole class. Children remain at their desk for most of the teaching sessions and many of the tasks are designed for individual study rather than for groups of children working together. Although the tables can be placed together for activities when necessary, you should consider whether the benefits of grouping children outweigh the disadvantages caused through off-task talk and distractions. A formal setting facilitates individual learning. By contrast, genuine collaborative work is hindered by a formal arrangement of furniture.

Each layout provides some helpful permanent resources (such as sinks), unhelpful fixtures (such as too much furniture inside the main room) and, from the positioning of tables and other furniture, clues about the way in which the context might influence lesson design and application.

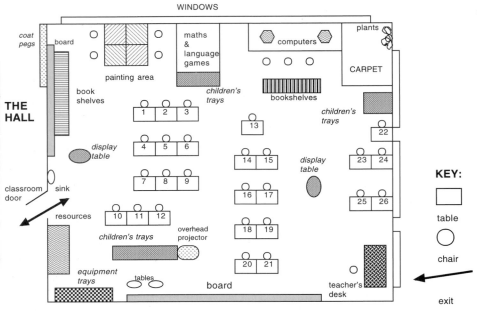

Figure 5.6 Classroom layout 1

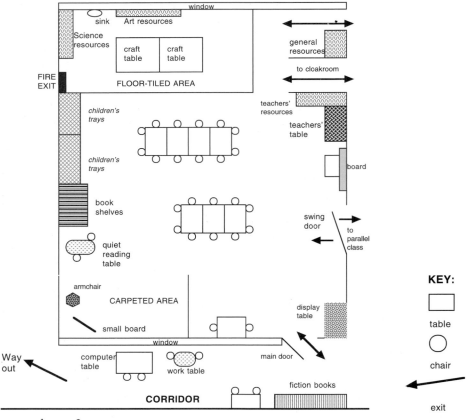

Figure 5.7 Classroom layout 2

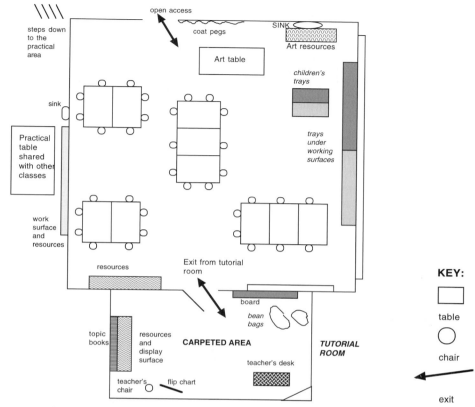

Figure 5.8 Classroom layout 3

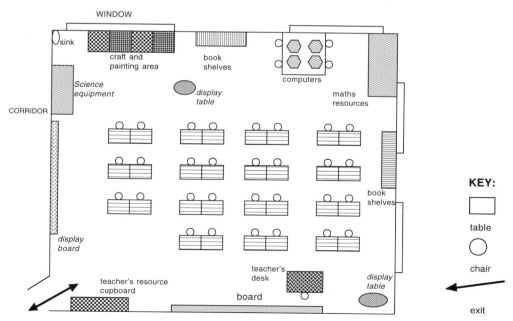

Figure 5.9 Classroom layout 4

The impact of your lessons

CASE STUDY

Seven year-old Kelly likes her class teacher, Mrs Thorne, but still looks forward to different adults teaching her. One day, you turn up in the classroom and begin to work with her group on how to write a book review. Kelly has never met you before and wonders what you are like. You have prepared your lesson very carefully, timed the lesson's phases (introduction; main teaching; review; clearing-up) and feel confident that it will be a success. At the end of the time, the children have completed their reviews of well-loved books based on the basic idea that you presented, and you feel pleased with quality of the results. One of the children asks you if you will be teaching them again; you respond by saying that you expect to do so. The children disappear for break and the class teacher enquires about the lesson. You are excited about what you achieved and the teacher encourages you by praising your efforts. But how successful *was* the lesson; and how do you know?

Success will have depended upon three things: 1) the thoroughness of your preparation; 2) the appropriateness of the lesson; 3) the impact the lesson had on children like Kelly. Let's look at some of the issues by contrasting two versions of what happened:

- you were excited about the lesson and this transmitted to Kelly *or*
- you were excited but Kelly was thinking 'we've done this lots of times before';

- you and Kelly were happy with the writing that she produced *or*
- Kelly was secretly scornful of your enthusiastic praise, knowing that she could have done much better;

- you were pleased when Kelly asked you eagerly if you were going to teach them again *or*
- you missed the tone in Kelly's voice which intimated that she hoped that you were *not* going to do so as the last lesson was unfulfilling;

- you and Kelly were looking forward to the next lesson with anticipation *or*
- neither of you had given much thought to what comes next.

EVALUATING YOUR LESSONS

Every college has a requirement that students evaluate their lessons in some way to review their own role as a teacher, the children's learning, and the organisation involved. Lesson reviews are an opportunity for students to reflect and consider significant aspects of their teaching as a pointer for future improvements and development. Evaluating lessons is important because just as children learn, you are also learning ... about your teaching. It is important to realise that teaching is far more than a mechanistic process. It requires qualities like judgement, speed of thought, rapid response and an understanding of the way in which children act and think. Some students tend to make rather woolly remarks in their lesson reviews such as 'This was a good lesson ...' but reviews should be more specific and pin-point aspects of the lesson or lessons which were noteworthy and where improvements might be possible or desirable in future lessons. They also help you to assess your own progress against criteria that the college will provide for you. In your evaluations, it is common to focus on one of three areas:

The extent to which your lesson intentions were achieved
Using evidence from children's responses, the quality of the work, the breadth of their thinking, or their understanding as shown through answers to your questions.
Specific teaching skills
See Chapter 6.
Common events and incidents
Focusing on particular classroom episodes such as what happened during different stages of the lesson, distribution of resources, giving feed back, group problem solving and so on, can highlight issues such as the need to clarify your expectations, strategies for maintaining reasonable noise levels, matching of work with ability, the behaviour of individual children, the depth of your planning and managing more than one group at a time. Use your reaction to events, your overall teaching approach. Your written evaluation should acknowledge the positive contribution that the episode has made to your thinking and development as a teacher.

Performance indicators
The benchmarks that you use to determine whether your lessons have achieved what you purposed are known as *performance indicators*. There are three types:

1) ATTITUDINAL
You judge success by the level of children's enthusiasm, contributions and involvement in the lessons. Poor attitudes indicate that your teaching has been inappropriate or uninspiring. The more carefully you prepare interesting and suitable lessons, the more likely that children will do their best and achieve high standards. You cannot hope to get things right every lesson, but by paying close attention to children's reactions, comments and effort, and adjusting your lessons as a result, you can improve their attitude to learning.

CASE STUDY

At the end of your drama session on 'Trusting', in which you use a series of blind-folding activities, the children talk excitedly about what they have done and ask you if they can do some more next time. Several groups tell you that they are going to make up some ideas of their own during the playtime. You warn them to be careful not to fall over if they do so!

NOTE: Good teaching inspires children to learn more.

Attitudinal performance indicator . . . You have succeeded in enthusing the class and cultivating a positive attitude towards drama.
Implications . . . Consider using some of the children's ideas in future lessons. Opportunities should exist for transferring the collaborative culture from the hall session into classroom work and thereby enhancing your relationship with the class.
Further development . . . If you establish classroom discussion after the lesson or ask for written comments about the impact of the lessons, you will gain more insight into individual attitudes.

2) CRITERION REFERENCED

This performance indicator uses the criteria that you have established for judging success. Unless you are teaching children of uniform ability, you will establish more demanding criteria for tasks undertaken by children of higher ability. At the end of the teaching phase, you can assess the quality of the children's work by reference to these criteria.

CASE STUDY

NOTE: Pay close attention to children's innovative ideas. Children usually have a good reason for their actions if you take the trouble to ask them. Be careful that one child does not become a sleeping partner.

Your new entrants are working with a variety of two-dimensional shapes. After your initial explanation, pairs of children have the task of putting the shapes into sets.
Criterion referenced performance indicators . . . As you observe the children at work, you take note of three criteria: a) the accuracy of their decisions; b) their explanations about why they have taken those decisions; c) their willingness to consider alternative groupings to the obvious ones.
Implications . . .

- The children may carry out the task correctly, yet lack essential *vocabulary* to describe what they are doing.
- They may place objects in a way which is apparently incorrect, yet have a *rational explanation* for their actions.
- The task may be completed based on the understanding of only *one* child rather than both.

Further development ... The range of responses need to be discussed with all the children, allowing every child to become more familiar with essential terminology and explore other creative possibilities.

▲▲

3) NORM REFERENCED

Norm referenced indicators are applicable when children are being compared with one another and where there is a previously determined standard for children of that age. The most common example is when the same spelling test is given to every child and a mark awarded. The results indicate children's differing competence to spell single words out of context. Standardised tests and tasks that use a marking sheet and result in a grade being awarded to every child are norm referenced. Norm referenced indicators are useful in establishing criteria for use with different ability groups, but need to be carried out under closely supervised conditions if they are to be valid.

CASE STUDY

▼▼▼▼▼▼▼▼▼▼▼▼▼▼▼▼   ▼▼▼▼▼▼▼▼▼▼▼▼▼▼▼

You give your class of ten year-olds a formal multiplication test, easier ones first; more demanding ones last.

Norm referenced performance indicator ... Final marks range from 4 out of 20 to 20 out of 20. The standardised norm for the age group of children is 15 out of 20. As the class average falls below this score (13 out of 20), you conclude that children with marks below the standardised score need remedial help.

Implications ... The results are a little disappointing. However, on careful examination of the test papers, you notice several interesting trends:

- **Some children got most of the first ten questions correct and most of the final ten incorrect.**
- **Although some children got most of those they attempted correct, they left puzzling blanks from time to time when those particular questions were no harder than the preceding ones.**
- **Some children appeared to have put the correct answers opposite the wrong number question.**

Further development ... It is clear that for some children, it would have been appropriate for them to attempt only the first ten questions, in which case their mark would have been 10 out of 10 rather than (say) twelve out of twenty. The children who had the puzzling blanks were obviously those who could work out the

NOTE: Norm-referenced testing is not as straightforward as it appears. Although a bare test result gives some useful information, it is important to ensure that it accurately reflects the child's ability and understanding, and is not viewed in isolation from other evidence about children's understanding.

NOTE: attitudinal indicators apply most readily to creative activities, criteria referenced indicators to work in foundation subjects and topic work, and norm referenced to core areas. As you reflect upon your performance as a teacher, careful use of indicators such as these can enhance your teaching by giving you a clearer picture of the children's progress.

answers, but rather slower than was required for the test; consequently, they missed out the odd question as they tried to keep pace. Finally, some children knew certain answers but were too disorganized or anxious to write the answers in the proper place; in the same way as the puzzled children, their final mark did not reflect their ability

▲▲▲

Comments from teachers

In addition to the supervisor's comments, the class teacher and other school staff often make useful and informed comments about your teaching. It is worth noting in a log or diary some of the key points that they raise informally. Over the period of the school experience, these build up into a useful portfolio of suggestions which could be incorporated into your Personal Development Portfolio (PDP). Teachers are impressed when students write down the points they make and the advice they offer. Later, as you reflect upon the teacher's comment, you can write your own response to it and build up a valuable resource for future action. This process not only focuses your thinking on important issues of classroom practice, but gives you an insight into the educational philosophy and priorities of serving teachers.

Lesson preparation is a complex operation. The best lessons are linked with National Curriculum expectations, the school's own plans and the classroom context. Your own reflections, guided and enhanced by other people's informed comments, assist in the process of evaluating and improving your teaching.

CHAPTER 6

Teaching Performance

> **Good teachers, it is commonly held, are keen and enthusiastic, well organised, firm but fair, stimulating, know their stuff, and are interested in the welfare of their pupils**
>
> *(Dunne and Wragg, 1994)*

There are almost as many teaching approaches as there are teachers. The individual nature of teaching partly explains its attraction as a profession to so many people. The opportunity to express yourself creatively and develop enterprising strategies to support children's learning is hugely rewarding. A number of educationists have watched teachers at work and tried to group them according to their teaching style, but efforts to do so have rarely proved satisfactory. Nevertheless, qualities like enthusiasm, dedication and clarity of purpose in teachers are found to be essential if their pupils are to fulfil their potential.

As a guest in the school, your own style of teaching will have to reflect the class teacher's style to some extent. In doing so, you must always take account of your own priorities, and evaluate whether your teaching intentions are reflected in the children's progress.

Although you cannot force children to learn anything, you can strongly encourage them to do so by providing suitable conditions in which your lessons take place:

- *Security:* in which mistakes are accepted, effort is acknowledged and enquiring minds are valued;
- *Motivation:* in which the end result is worth the children's efforts and they enjoy what they are doing;
- *Celebration:* in which there is a spirit of enterprise, children are encouraged to value the efforts of others, and achievements are publicly recognised.

Effective teaching can be defined as that which enables children to fulfil their learning potential. The way in which you manage your teaching plays an essential role in achieving this.

MANAGING YOUR TEACHING

The first teaching experience for many students consists of working with a small number of children in one of the core subject areas. Over time, the extent of their responsibility widens to include several groups and the whole class. Whatever stage you have reached in your school experience, your task is to ensure that your classroom organisation is simple enough for you to manage, yet designed in such a way that children are working at a level appropriate to their abilities. The class teacher will help you to make wise decisions about these matters.

There are three levels of teaching responsibility that may be required of you (see Figure 6.1). If you are given just **one group** of children, you may teach them a lesson that you have specially prepared for them or one activity out of a number that the whole class eventually have to cover. Later in your teaching experience, you may plan **a lesson for the whole class**, in which case the more able will work through the early stages of the lesson with relative ease, whereas the less able may not progress too far. In such a case, it is important to have an open-ended task for all the children once they have completed as much of the formal work as they can (see Figure 6.2 opposite). When you have gained a lot of teaching experience, you will be asked to take responsibility for the whole class and provide **different types of tasks and activities** for different groups of children, according to their ability.

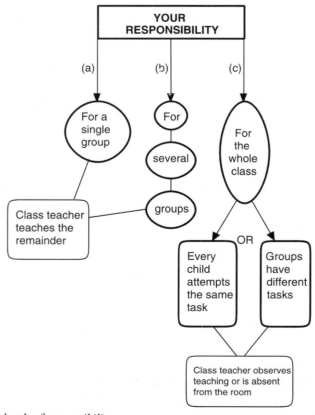

Figure 6.1 Three levels of responsibility

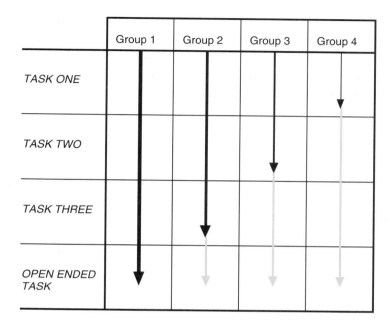

	Group 1	Group 2	Group 3	Group 4
TASK ONE				
TASK TWO				
TASK THREE				
OPEN ENDED TASK				

Group 1 completes tasks smoothly and quickly engages with the open ended task

Group 2 completes the tasks with effort and moves forward into the open ended task

Group 3 only completes the first two tasks and is moved forward to the open ended task with teacher support

Group 4 completes the first task with teacher support and is moved to an amended version of the open ended task

Figure 6.2 Managing several groups engaged on the same task

Some students find it hard to transfer their skills from working with a single group to responsibility for the whole class because working with a single group means giving a few children exclusive attention. With responsibility for the whole class, it is difficult to attend to a single group and at the same time keep an eye on other areas of the room. Teaching the whole class does not necessarily mean that all the children are involved in the same activity. Indeed, it is unusual for all children of the same age to tackle identical work due to their different abilities and levels of understanding.

If you have several groups or the whole class to manage, you need to develop the practice of **surveying** the room at regular intervals to monitor what is happening and avoid the situation in which you become so involved with a small number of children that you neglect all the others. An occasional hard stare at any children who are unsettled, and well-judged hand signals to those children who need attention, will minimise the need to scurry from one place to another in an attempt to deal with children's questions, queries and restlessness. You will, however, have to be alert to what is happening throughout the room, decisive in preventing problems from arising, and firm in dealing with those that do. The more that you can develop your presence in the room, the more aware you will be of what is happening, and the more sensitive you will become to gauging the length of time you need to spend with different children. Concentrate on developing a 'crow's nest view', in which you are always alert to what is happening around you (Figure 6.3).

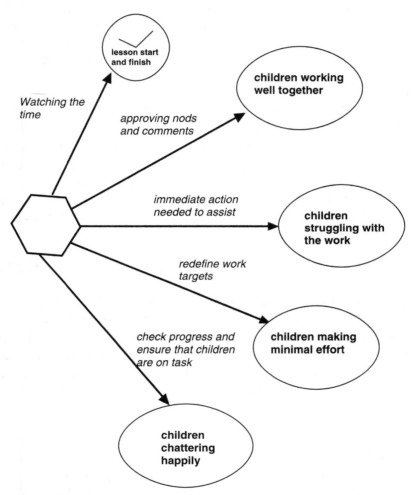

Figure 6.3 A crow's nest view of the classroom

Teaching approaches
In broad terms, there are three available teaching approaches that you can use:

1) TELLING THE CHILDREN WHAT THEY NEED TO KNOW
The children are inactive recipients of the information that you are giving to them, but this does not mean that telling them things has to be monotonous or uninspiring. Your

variation of tone, good eye contact, interesting questions and enthusiasm, can transform a potentially uninteresting session into one which captivates and motivates. Of course, it is important to ensure that the children are paying close attention to what you are saying, and you may wish to ask questions after you have finished your explanation to check whether the children have grasped what you tried to tell them. Children should be encouraged to think about what you are saying, even if they are not engaged in practical activities. Pye (1987) warns that when addressing the whole class, teachers fail to involve some children or make eye contact with them. This creates a sub-group of marginalised children who do not interact with the teacher, hear what is said, or have much interest in what is happening. Watch out for any such children in your class and ensure that you involve them, too.

2) THE CHILDREN FINDING OUT FOR THEMSELVES WHAT THEY NEED TO KNOW

Children investigate a problem to which there is an answer or a variety of answers. Children are often put into pairs or grouped for this purpose. You must first ensure that children possess the necessary study skills and strategies to facilitate the task of finding out. Sometimes, you may want to give the children some information and then set them the task of confirming what you have said, finding alternatives or discovering more about a topic.

3) THE CHILDREN WORKING SEQUENTIALLY THROUGH SET TEXTS OR A SCHEME

You provide essential information about the work through explanation or demonstration, and the text acts as a test of their understanding or reinforcement of something already learned. Text books are more often used in Maths and aspects of English than in the foundation subjects. It is unwise to rely too heavily on a text, which should be seen as a support for your teaching rather than a substitute teacher. If children are using texts ask yourself whether they are using the text to practice what they already understand, extend their understanding, or explore new ground.

Age of children

Teaching approaches need to take account of the children's age and progress. For instance, older children are normally better at retaining facts after being told; younger ones will learn less by being told but more by experiencing through touching, tasting, interacting with, exploring, being amazed by, asking questions about, repeating, and so on. Older children develop the ability to think abstractly using their minds without the need for concrete supporting aids; younger ones require time to reinforce concepts through handling and manipulating objects. For younger children, in particular, seeing is believing, though less confident older primary children may rely on visual aids for longer than they are really required. Thus, even children towards the top of a primary school may continue using their fingers for counting, look up simple and familiar words in a dictionary, and spend time drawing pictures rather than writing. These habits often signal a lack of self belief rather than lack of ability. All children benefit from relevant, interesting lessons.

Interesting ideas

Children respond positively if you can transform everyday activities into exciting ones. To do this you have to use your imagination. For example, a common activity like mapping out the school grounds could, depending upon the age and ability of the children, be developed as a mock TV presentation (later to be presented in front of another class) or a brochure for visitors. Younger children can be encouraged to imagine that they have never been in the place before and act out some drama. Opportunities for wearing simple costumes, designating areas of the room for particular purposes (as a castle, medieval forest, word world, moon crater, toy land, or whatever), going back in time, and other variations on the theme, can raise interest levels and create incentives for learning. It is not possible to be fabulously enterprising for every session of the day, but imaginative teaching is often the hallmark of a confident and effective teacher.

Individual and special needs

All children have their own particular needs. The more you know about individuals, the better you become in organising their work, responding to their concerns and anticipating their problems. In addition, there will always be some children who have needs which are substantially different from the majority. Children with Special Educational Needs will already have been identified by the class teacher and classified according to the severity of that need. Under the most severe circumstances, children may have additional support from another adult, and follow an Individual Education Plan of activities geared to their needs. During your time in school, you should be familiar with these cases and aware of children's limitations and potential, including how the learning of *more able* children can be extended.

Involving pupils in their learning

Whatever approach or combination of approaches you take, it is essential that the children *engage* with their learning. That is, they understand what is required of them, and are sufficiently interested in the work to persevere with the tasks that you have set. Some children complete work without ever using their brains properly by relying on someone else to do the thinking for them; others make minimal effort to achieve a satisfactory end product when they were capable of something much better. As you get to know the class better and become more confident, you will learn to ask children for their opinions, prompt them to express ideas, and respond positively to their idealism. In this way, the children take more ownership and responsibility for their learning. However, as children become enthusiastic about promoting their own ideas, you may have to resist some of their wackier suggestions!

Sharing findings

One way of enhancing children's active engagement with the work is to organise it in such a way that there is opportunity for them to share their ideas and findings with others in the class or children from another class. There are various ways in which this can be done:

- **The group produces an OHP sheet with key points listed on it.**
- **The group performs a short mime.**
- **As a result of the group's investigations, other children are invited to write comments on sheets pinned up around the room, responding (say) to a question written at the top of each sheet. (Note, however, the potential for excess noise and disruption as children move about).**
- **The group takes a poll of opinions from the rest of the class before and after presenting their findings about a topic of interest.**
- **Older children go into a class of younger children to share pictures, stories and drama.**

These approaches require advanced organisation and careful planning, but they offer interesting variations in the ways that children can record and present their own findings.

Reporting back can be logistically demanding. You will have to allow for the possibility that some groups will finish before others. The *process* of reporting is not always easy to handle, either. Very young children may not be used to recording their findings in different ways or sharing with their classmates. Older ones may use the opportunity to over elaborate or cause some mischief by taking advantage of the freedom offered to them. You will need to impress upon the groups the need for strict time management and courtesy in listening to others. It is helpful to ask children to have a question to put to the reporting group after listening to their presentation. In the early days of working in this way, groups usually need considerable support and guidance, but children learn to be innovative and self-sufficient surprisingly quickly, and will soon be suggesting all sorts of variations. Lessons do not always have to conclude with 'now write it down'!

Investigating and exploring

Lessons in which the children are encouraged to find out for themselves need to take account of what they already know and understand. The worst kind of lesson is one in which children are asked to find out as much as they can about something without being given clearly specified targets and strategies for going about it. When children are first engaged in discovering facts for themselves, it may be tempting for you to approve of what they do regardless of the quality of work. However, in your desire to encourage children to show enterprise and initiative, you must not let them loose to wander at will like grazing cattle. The results of this casual approach are often disappointing and do not lead to enriched learning. It is much more productive to set targets for learning that you and the children can monitor, otherwise investigative activities degenerate into time fillers, and ultimately time wasters, which serve little educational purpose. For instance, you may ask the children to *find out* about an historical character such as Napoleon. But what are they engaged in learning about? Possibilities include:

- **his career path**
- **the battles he fought and lost**
- **the colour of his underpants!**

Without guidance from you, children will spend too much time aimlessly flicking through unsuitable books that are difficult to read, and copying a few pictures of Napoleon gazing out across the battlefield at the carnage below. Although tracing and colouring will keep the children happy for a time, you will feel dissatisfied with the end product. A simple assessment of what the children have learned (apart from how to colour) will probably show that they have gained little from the time they have spent on their investigations. Disappointment and wasted time can be avoided if purposes are initially identified, such as:

- **the reasons for Napoleon becoming a general in the first place;**
- **what factors made him so successful in battle;**
- **how his defeat came about;**
- **his importance as a historical figure.**

The success of the lesson depends upon what it is you want the children to learn or understand. You may want to compare the qualities of Napoleon and the Duke of Wellington, or to concentrate on the geography of the region in which the battles were fought, or to promote a discussion about the futility of war. The process of *finding out* has to be made specific and purposeful.

All the children in the class do not have to find out exactly the same things. It is better to divide the class into groups and allow each group to explore a different aspect of the topic before holding the reporting back session so that everyone can benefit from hearing about what others have found.

Investigating is a powerful means of organising for learning, but it will prove counter-productive if viewed as an easy option. You may as well have used much simpler teaching strategies such as providing the whole class with a prepared worksheet, teaching from the front or using a question-and-answer approach. However, it pays to persevere with investigative and exploratory activities. Shared experiences of this sort are often the richest.

Use of worksheets

Worksheets are commonly used by students and qualified teachers for two reasons: they can be prepared in advance and they provide an outline lesson structure. They are normally used individually or in pairs by children who are seated, thereby minimising the possibility of disruption through wandering about. They can be designed in such a way that they keep a group of children occupied without much teacher support, thereby releasing you to work closely with other groups. In a classroom in which there are several different activities taking place, it is likely that at least one group will be occupied with a worksheet.

However, there are important questions that you need to ask yourself before distributing your much-loved work of art:

- **What is its purpose?**
- **How does it fit in with other work?**
- **Are children learning anything as a result of doing it?**
- **How will you introduce it, monitor children's progress and evaluate the outcome?**

Worksheets need to be clearly written without too much detail on a single sheet. Depending upon their purpose, they should contain necessary information, directions about what is required of the children, and supporting advice about resources, strategies or techniques for completing the work. You should also consider whether

- **the worksheet is self-explanatory, requiring little introduction;**
- **the worksheet contains unusual or difficult vocabulary;**
- **the worksheet is best completed by children working independently, or by pairs, or by groups.**

Every worksheet should be numbered or identifiable in some way (such as a simple code number in the top right hand corner) to help you keep track of them and store them systematically. The best ones contain sections requiring the children to exercise a variety of thinking skills: mastery of information, practice, speculation, problem-solving and so on. Although a single worksheet cannot contain everything, it is surprising what you can achieve with a little imagination. If you want to re-use your sheets, print them on card instead of paper, and place them in transparent plastic covers.

Figures 6.4 and 6.5 on pages 86 and 87 are examples of worksheets which might be used with a Key Stage 2 theme based on 'The Victorians'. Notice that although the main thrust of the worksheet focuses on aspects of historical facts, there are also elements of Maths and Geography included. Part of the worksheet is for individual work, and part of it requires children to work with a partner. If you used a worksheet of this type, you need to consider a number of logistical factors:

- **the practicalities of a child who had worked on his or her own initially, being matched with a suitable partner for the later sections;**
- **the availability of suitable atlases;**
- **the noise generated during the discussions;**
- **the way in which children will gain access to other information sources;**
- **your own availability should a child require assistance.**

Worksheets are sometimes over-used by teachers, but if considered as one teaching strategy to be used in combination with others, they offer opportunities to enhance children's learning across a range of subject areas.

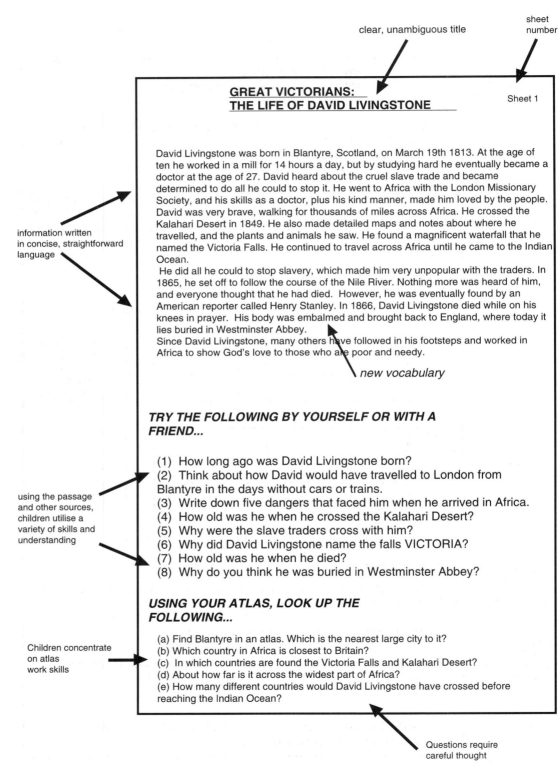

clear, unambiguous title

sheet number

GREAT VICTORIANS:
THE LIFE OF DAVID LIVINGSTONE

Sheet 1

David Livingstone was born in Blantyre, Scotland, on March 19th 1813. At the age of ten he worked in a mill for 14 hours a day, but by studying hard he eventually became a doctor at the age of 27. David heard about the cruel slave trade and became determined to do all he could to stop it. He went to Africa with the London Missionary Society, and his skills as a doctor, plus his kind manner, made him loved by the people. David was very brave, walking for thousands of miles across Africa. He crossed the Kalahari Desert in 1849. He also made detailed maps and notes about where he travelled, and the plants and animals he saw. He found a magnificent waterfall that he named the Victoria Falls. He continued to travel across Africa until he came to the Indian Ocean.

He did all he could to stop slavery, which made him very unpopular with the traders. In 1865, he set off to follow the course of the Nile River. Nothing more was heard of him, and everyone thought that he had died. However, he was eventually found by an American reporter called Henry Stanley. In 1866, David Livingstone died while on his knees in prayer. His body was embalmed and brought back to England, where today it lies buried in Westminster Abbey.

Since David Livingstone, many others have followed in his footsteps and worked in Africa to show God's love to those who are poor and needy.

information written in concise, straightforward language

new vocabulary

TRY THE FOLLOWING BY YOURSELF OR WITH A FRIEND...

(1) How long ago was David Livingstone born?
(2) Think about how David would have travelled to London from Blantyre in the days without cars or trains.
(3) Write down five dangers that faced him when he arrived in Africa.
(4) How old was he when he crossed the Kalahari Desert?
(5) Why were the slave traders cross with him?
(6) Why did David Livingstone name the falls VICTORIA?
(7) How old was he when he died?
(8) Why do you think he was buried in Westminster Abbey?

using the passage and other sources, children utilise a variety of skills and understanding

USING YOUR ATLAS, LOOK UP THE FOLLOWING...

(a) Find Blantyre in an atlas. Which is the nearest large city to it?
(b) Which country in Africa is closest to Britain?
(c) In which countries are found the Victoria Falls and Kalahari Desert?
(d) About how far is it across the widest part of Africa?
(e) How many different countries would David Livingstone have crossed before reaching the Indian Ocean?

Children concentrate on atlas work skills

Questions require careful thought

Figure 6.4 Worksheet Example 1

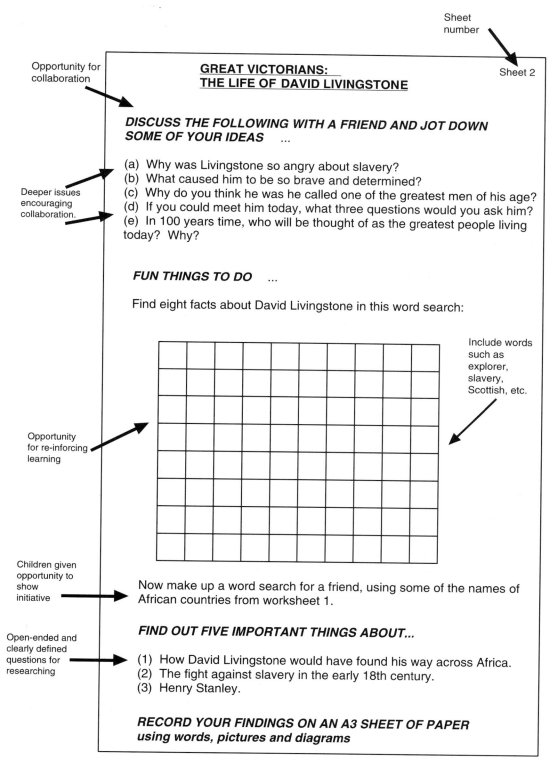

Sheet
number

Opportunity for
collaboration

GREAT VICTORIANS:
THE LIFE OF DAVID LIVINGSTONE

Sheet 2

DISCUSS THE FOLLOWING WITH A FRIEND AND JOT DOWN
SOME OF YOUR IDEAS   ...

(a) Why was Livingstone so angry about slavery?
(b) What caused him to be so brave and determined?
(c) Why do you think he was he called one of the greatest men of his age?
(d) If you could meet him today, what three questions would you ask him?
(e) In 100 years time, who will be thought of as the greatest people living today? Why?

Deeper issues
encouraging
collaboration.

FUN THINGS TO DO   ...

Find eight facts about David Livingstone in this word search:

Include words
such as
explorer,
slavery,
Scottish, etc.

Opportunity
for re-inforcing
learning

Now make up a word search for a friend, using some of the names of African countries from worksheet 1.

Children given
opportunity to
show
initiative

FIND OUT FIVE IMPORTANT THINGS ABOUT...

(1) How David Livingstone would have found his way across Africa.
(2) The fight against slavery in the early 18th century.
(3) Henry Stanley.

Open-ended and
clearly defined
questions for
researching

RECORD YOUR FINDINGS ON AN A3 SHEET OF PAPER
using words, pictures and diagrams

Figure 6.5 Worksheet Example 2

TEACHING SKILLS

All trainee teachers need to master basic teaching skills; qualified teachers need to continue their development throughout their careers. Though the refinement of teaching skills does not guarantee good teaching, their absence is an impossible handicap. It is worth spending time in developing and perfecting your basic teaching skills. Make it your aim to achieve the highest possible standards and avoid bad habits, as these are not easily unlearned. Concentration on the following four skills will give you a strong advantage in your teaching:

- **correct use of the voice;**
- **clear explanations;**
- **asking appropriate questions;**
- **assessment, recording and reporting.**

Correct use of the voice

The importance of clear speech and proper care of the voice cannot be over-emphasised. Many students get throat problems due to strain caused by improper use and exposure to common classroom germs, so you need to treat your throat and larynx with the same sort of care and attention that an opera singer might do. The small amount of attention given to speech training in college courses is due to

- **the trend towards organising learning through dividing into small group activities rather than whole class, thereby reducing the need to project the voice;**
- **the growing use of non-verbal strategies for class control (for instance, using eye contact and hand gestures) compared with voice commands.**

All teachers need to speak clearly and naturally, yet without shouting. It is worth cultivating good habits:

SPEAK NATURALLY

Try to speak without forcing your voice or tightening your throat and facial muscles .

BREATHE REGULARLY

In stressful situations, many people actually forget to breathe. Practise breathing in through your nose, pausing and allowing your breath to flow evenly as you speak.

ARTICULATE YOUR WORDS

Children take time to adjust to the pitch and cadence of your voice. By speaking slowly at the start of a sentence and allowing your tongue and lips to move freely, you will be more likely to be heard first time. Pay particular attention to the sound of consonants, and avoid slurring the last letter of one word into the first letter of the next.

PAUSE BETWEEN STATEMENTS

Inexperienced or exuberant students sometimes get carried away in the excitement of teaching and fail to allow children time to absorb one statement before they are half-way into the next. Occasional short pauses, together with good eye contact across the class, reduces verbal overload.

TAKE ACCOUNT OF ACOUSTICS

In a large space, echoes and reverberations can affect voice clarity. Generally, the larger the space the slower you need to speak. In addition, the more people in a given space the more the sound is absorbed, and the more carefully your words need to be articulated.

KEEP GOOD ORDER

You can minimise voice strain by ensuring that every child is listening before you begin speaking. If you have a lot to say in a hall or gymnasium, it is worth sitting the children in one corner to address them all, rather than attempting to make yourself heard by scattered individuals. The need for discipline is particularly important during potentially hazardous activities such as swimming and large-scale apparatus work, when a command has to be obeyed instantly.

In the classroom, your voice has to fulfil many roles in explaining, warning, confirming, encouraging, rebuking, clarifying, praising and so on. Each of these requires a slightly different use of the voice. Children are affected by the various tones you use. For instance, if you slow your voice considerably and speak in a staccato manner with slightly longer pauses between words than normal, children discern that you expect them to pay close attention. A sing-songy voice indicates to them that you are in a relaxed frame of mind! A warning normally involves a deepening of the voice, whereas praise involves raising the pitch.

Without correct use of the voice, the important skill of *speaking strongly* can deteriorate into shouting, with adverse effects upon your health and the classroom atmosphere. As a rule, use your voice like a glider rather than a battering ram or a cannon.

Clear explanations

Telling is not the same as explaining. You will know how embarrassing it is when someone has told you the same thing many times and cannot understand why you cannot grasp it. Children have similar feelings when a teacher becomes exasperated because they fail to understand something which, to the teacher, is obvious. It is important to improve your explanations in three areas:

EXPLAINING HOW

There are times when certain procedures or orders have to be followed and your explanation of *how* provides a blueprint for children to copy. In subsequent discussion with the children you may encourage them to offer alternative methods or suggestions for improvement; but your initial explanation (normally followed by a period of opportunity for the children to practice the skill) shows how something can or should be done. Explaining how also requires that you are clear in your own mind about the correct way to do things and can actively demonstrate it to the children. In explaining how, it is important to make it clear when you are offering the technique or approach as a good example, and when you are insisting that it is the only acceptable method. For instance, there may be several possible ways to vary the pitch of an elastic band, but only one way of playing a particular note on a recorder.

EXPLAINING WHAT

Every teacher spends a lot of time explaining *what* is expected of children. For instance, what work they have to complete, what standards of behaviour are required, what the day's programme will be. Such explanations often require further visual support to reinforce the message or act as a reminder of previous explanations. Explaining what can be supported by printed sheets of instructions, notes on a board, or memorising by rote. For instance, explaining what has to be done in the event of a fire is strengthened by having a bold list of instructions on the wall. Explaining what is meant by a certain word can be accompanied by examples of the use of the word in a sentence, pictures of scenes in which it is relevant, and so on. The explanation of what happens or what something means is thereby enhanced when accompanied by other visual stimuli.

EXPLAINING WHY

Explanations about how and what both require forward planning, careful thought and clear communication of ideas. Explaining *why* is more difficult as it can involve value judgements and sensitive issues. Some children ask for explanations about why something is necessary or why it happened because they are genuinely interested; others because they have adopted the practice of questioning everything that is said. Normally, the genuine questioner uses a natural tone, maintains eye contact with you, and nods at your reply. The subversive questioner, on the other hand, will normally avoid your gaze, respond negatively without bothering to listen to you and use a strained voice tone.

Explanations about why circumstances in life occur in the way they do, or about people's behaviour in society, or issues of unfairness, require careful handling. It pays to remember that a child usually has a reason for asking a why question, so try to ascertain the reason before attempting an explanation. Explaining why puzzling things happen is sometimes most successfully accomplished through a whole class discussion. Children also have to be taught to appreciate that there are also some questions about life that defy a simple explanation.

Asking appropriate questions

We have already seen that questions form an important part of the teaching process. As the teacher, you have a responsibility to engage children's minds and excite their interest by using relevant and suitable questions as a way of promoting learning (see Fisher, 1995, Chapter 2 for a helpful discussion of questioning). A worthwhile question is one that children can understand, see its relevance for their lives, and excite their curiosity. It is important to write down your questions as part of your lesson planning. Good questions encourage children to extend their thinking, probe their uncertainties and open up new worlds of understanding. Even when there appears to be an apparently simple answer to a straightforward question, you can help children to reconstruct their ideas and advance their thinking by asking questions which begin with phrases like:

- **What do you think she felt like when . . . ?**
- **What if he hadn't looked there . . . ?**
- **Can you think of another way it might have ended . . . ?**
- **Is it right to do it that way . . . ?**
- **What other endings to the story are possible . . . ?**
- **Why do some people behave that way . . . ?**
- **What would you have said if you had been the girl . . . ?**

Four main types of questions are used by teachers.

- **Read my mind questions**
- **Open questions**
- **Opinions**
- **Speculation**

READ MY MIND QUESTIONS

Use this type of questioning sparingly. If there is a single correct answer, it is often easier for you to *tell* the children rather than indulge in a pointless exercise in which you ask child after child until eventually you receive the correct answer or are forced to tell them because no-one knows. For instance, children will either know or not know that the capital of France is Paris. If it is important for them to know, tell them about Paris in an entertaining and memorable way that will help to establish the fact firmly in their memories. For instance, ask how many words they can think of that rhyme with Paris; make other words from the word Paris; show the position of Paris on a map; ask about holidays in France, and so on. Telling children facts does not have to be a dry and lifeless exercise; use your imagination and extend theirs.

OPEN-ENDED QUESTIONS

If there are a variety of possible answers to a question, invite the children to provide suggestions. For instance, if you ask them to tell you the colour of the sky, a few children will doubtless answer that it is blue; others will disagree and say that the sky is grey or red or purple. You can use these different responses as a basis for talking about weather patterns, atmospheric conditions, seasons of the year, or whatever is appropriate to the children's age and ability. Open-ended questions of this type are a powerful entrance to learning; however, you must make sure that you have anticipated the likely reponses beforehand and thought about the comments that you will make and the overall purpose of the interaction.

OPINIONS

Some questions ask children to consider various options and comment upon their merit. For instance, you may want to ask the opinion of your group of six year-olds about whether the pencils should be kept in a central block in the middle of the table or separately in trays, or ask them their opinion about the rights and wrongs of leaving food uneaten at lunchtime, as a means of stimulating interest in issues of fairness, good eating habits or nutrition. It can be helpful to gain a class view of how to ensure that games, toys and puzzles are shared, or that everyone has use of the computer, or that everyone sits still during the story. You are not escaping your responsibilities by asking opinions, but demonstrating to the children that they have both rights and responsibilities as members of the class or group. You still make the final decision, giving your reasons as you do so.

With older children, it is sometimes useful to split them into small groups to discuss the facts about issues before reporting their conclusions to other class members. Issues which have a moral dimension (such as injustice, misrepresentation or cheating) are usually of great interest to older children and often provide the spark for a fruitful discussion.

The most perceptive opinions result from a discussion of issues over which the children have some immediate control (such as fair use of classroom equipment) or those which are far off but have relevance for today (such as the hazards facing early explorers). You need to take more care with questions relating to current issues which are *beyond* the children's control, such as the plight of children in modern wars. Unwise attention to such issues can result in children experiencing frustration, guilt or anguish because of their own impotence. Nevertheless, children soon blossom when they are genuinely asked for their opinions, guided in their responses by a sensitive teacher who respects their views.

SPECULATION

In areas of the curriculum in which problems have to be solved, children can be encouraged to speculate about likely outcomes. Questions which demand the children to speculate may be cause and effect types, in which action A is linked directly with outcome B; or more abstract types, in which the scenario is unfamiliar or imaginary. Answers to questions in which there is *cause and effect* can sometimes be confirmed through experimentation. For example, children's ideas about which materials best conduct electricity from a battery can be fair tested to discover the correct answer. More *abstract* speculation takes longer to develop and may not be suitable for the very young, but it is useful in fostering collaboration through joint problem solving.

Older children can be presented with a case scenario and divided into groups to discuss and speculate about desirable or likely outcomes. A simple question about the impact on a world without electricity for a day, or the effect upon life if everyone became a metre taller, or the implications for the quality of life if everything were coloured grey, can pave the way for challenging and valuable insights into issues such as gratitude, suitability, thankfulness, the environment, and so forth. Many short stories or examples of personal experience can bring a freshness to your teaching and stimulate the children's responses. Speculating tends to focus children's minds on present realities in their quest to probe the range of possible solutions. More confident children can use their ideas for a class presentation or as the basis for an assembly.

As you ponder your questioning technique, remember that children also need to ask their *own* questions, either because they are genuinely curious about something or due to their insecurity and the need for the reassurance that comes from your answers. To a large extent, you can gauge the impact of your questioning skills by the extent to which the children increase the range and quality of their own questions.

Assessment, recording and reporting (AR and R)

Monitoring pupils' progress and offering appropriate feedback is one of the most important skills that teachers develop. To help you to determine how much assessment and feedback to give during a lesson, remember that there are three main types of assessment carried out by teachers:

- *formative* assessment concerned with helping children to improve their work in progress;
- *evaluative* assessment in which the quality of work is monitored as the lesson unfolds;
- *summative* assessment in which the finished product is considered.

Years ago, nearly all assessment was summative. Teachers used to set a piece of work, wait until the children had completed the task, collect in what they had done, mark it away from the classroom and return it with a grade or comment. Today's teacher tries to monitor work more closely and offer immediate formative feedback with the child present. Many useful and interesting insights are gained through the intimacy of formative assessment and feedback, which gives you opportunity to assess children's understanding, pinpoint the sort of confusions which may exist, offer explanations, share understanding and enter a helpful dialogue about the work. However, immediate feedback is time consuming and tiring, and you will have to decide how much time to spend on this form of feedback and how much the children work unaided until they have completed the task. Some children rely too heavily upon the teacher, lack confidence in their own ability and ask endless questions. Others need only occasional reassuring comments and work largely unaided.

You can provide formative feedback in various ways: spoken advice, written comments, ticks, nods of approval or disapproval or by providing exemplars. Each instance of feedback is intended to affect the way children work and improve their understanding, knowledge and skills in that subject area. Children are very sensitive to teachers' comments, so it is worth spending time considering your own approach. There are four main factors to consider in this aspect of monitoring children's work:

- the task in which the children are involved;
- the criteria for assessment that you have in mind;
- the signals that you give children about the quality of their work through your words and voice tone;
- the effect it has upon the child's application and attitude.

The task in which they are involved will affect the responses you give and the *vocabulary* of assessment that you use. For instance, you would be unlikely to use terms such as 'neat' and 'correct' if applied to a child's painting. Similarly, terms such as 'shade' and 'texture' would be inappropriate in a science experiment. The vocabulary of feedback is important because children need to understand the expressions used and be able to interpret their meaning. Consider the number of times a teacher says: 'That's not the right way to do it' when examining a piece of maths work; or 'You'll have to use a stronger colour' in art; or 'There isn't enough detail' in mapwork. Each of these expressions signifies different things:

- **'That's not the right way to do it, Parak' implies that only one method is acceptable.**
- **'You'll have to use a stronger colour, Beverley' indicates that the painting does not conform closely to the teacher's perceptions of the object.**
- **'There isn't enough detail, Chris' suggests that the map is insufficiently exact.**

However, the situation is more complex than it seems. In each example, the teacher is *defining her own expectations* closely. Thus, the sum had to be correctly answered by using a conventional solution; the life drawing had to be an exact replication of the original; the map had to fulfil a particular (unspecified) purpose. Although the teacher was imposing her assessment criteria in the light of the on-going work, by doing so she might have been unintentionally restricting the child's creativity. Thus, the child who had to work out the sum might have been doing it incorrectly or might have been devising his own creative solution. The child who used pale colours may have mixed the paints incorrectly or may have been experimenting with a different technique. The child whose map was light on detail may have misunderstood what was required from the teacher or may have wanted the map to serve a different function from the one the teacher intended. The teacher's feedback on the children's work needed to take account of these factors.

Formative assessment must enhance a child's learning and not detract from it. For instance, Parak may eventually have got the correct answer to the sum by using a conventional method but missed the opportunity to extend his thinking through applying his own method. Beverley's painting may have resembled the original more closely, but lost the special character that she intended. The map might have been completed with more symbols, but become unsuitable for the purpose for which Chris had hoped to use it.

A more effective method of assessing on-going work and giving feedback is to use questions as a means of establishing the true situation more accurately. Instead of the comments listed above, you could ask:

'This looks interesting Parak. Why have you done it that way?'
If you enquire gently and without threat, Parak will give you an honest answer. His answer will reveal that he doesn't understand, that he is trying something new, or that he has lost concentration. Depending on his response, your feedback could sound like this:

- *'Would you like me to explain it again to you?'*
- *'That's excellent. I'm pleased you're having a go. Let me know how you get on.'*
- *'I think it's worth starting again, don't you!'*

The next time in the lesson you engage with Parak, you can offer constructive feedback that helps him further his understanding, rather than offering a comment that leaves him without any framework or strategy for completing the task that he was endeavouring to accomplish.

And for the artwork:
'You've certainly made good progress on that painting, Beverley. What do you want it to look like when it's finished?'

And for the mapwork:
'Will your map be detailed enough for you to use it to find your way around, Chris?'

From the nature of the children's responses to your gentle probing, you should be able to determine whether your original instructions were sufficiently clear, and whether individual pupils are confused, inspired or disobedient. Your feedback acts as a spur for your own improvement as a teacher as well as the children's learning. Do not jump to conclusions about children's work patterns when assessing their achievements.

Lesson plans and assessment

Your lesson plans will be enhanced if you can include some reference to the standards of achievement you anticipate will be reached during the lesson. Thus:

- An *excellent* piece of work will have these qualities.
- A *good* piece of work will have these qualities.
- An *unsatisfactory* piece of work is likely to have these features.

For example, an **excellent** piece of written work may be neatly presented, clearly expressed and interesting to read. A **good** piece of work may be acceptably presented, understandable and make sense. An **unsatisfactory** piece of work will be difficult to read or understand. You may want to make these criteria even more explicit. For instance, the excellent piece of written work may have to be convincing and persuasive. The good piece of work may present a sensible argument. The unsatisfactory piece of work may be unconvincing and lack conviction. Similarly, the **excellent** drawing of an object could fulfil these criteria: the work is in perspective; the child has made appropriate use of shading; there is effective use of soft and hard pencils. A **good** grade for the same work might include: the drawing makes the object recognisable; there is some use of hard and soft shading; the drawing shows some awareness of perspective. An **unsatisfactory** piece would lack these essential features.

Two factors are important in drawing up criteria. First, a lot depends upon the amount of help and support the children are offered before and during the activity. Second, you have to decide whether the same criteria apply to every child. For example, it would be unreasonable to expect seven year-old's to produce a plan view of the classroom without previous instruction, practice and guidance in a variety of simpler situations (such as drawing a plan view of objects on their table top). The assessment criteria have to match the children's current experience and knowledge. Similarly, it would be entirely inappropriate to expect a child with poor co-ordination to complete a complex piece of weaving. You should develop the habit of setting children work targets that are reasonably within their grasp – not too easy, not too difficult – and monitoring their progress.

You must also take into account the *effort* a child has made in reaching an outcome. Two children may have reached a good standard, the one through exceptional effort, the other by coasting. The first child has achieved a good standard in respect of the whole class, but an exceptional personal standard. By contrast, the second child, though producing a piece of work of comparable standard, has under achieved.

An effort to include some reference to evaluating standards of children's work in your plans will help you to monitor progress and determine the success of your teaching. Such attention to detail also tends to reduce the use of feedback expressions such as 'That's nice' without any additional constructive comment. The Exemplification of Standards booklets produced by SCAA (1995) offer samples of children's work at different levels of achievement in the core subjects to use as a guide in assessing quality.

Teaching and assessment begins at the point when you check details from the PoS, through the stages of lesson delivery (which may take more than a single session to complete), to the lesson's conclusion, evaluation and assessment of children's progress. Note that if your assessment of the work's quality indicates underachievement or unsatisfactory results, you may need to offer further instruction and insist that the work is improved or repeated. Children who have completed the work successfully can be encouraged to extend their thinking and creativity through further opportunities (see Figure 6.6).

Recording your assessments can be a time-consuming task. As a trainee teacher, it is essential that you keep records which show the areas of the curriculum covered and the extent to which groups of children satisfactorily completed the work. If you monitor the progress of a sample of children, you can use the information to influence your future lesson planning. Pages of detailed records are only useful if they assist the teaching and learning. As a guide to the usefulness of records, consider how they might help you to inform parents about their children's progress, and how you would justify your judgements (see Hayes, 1996, Chapter 3).

> PARENTS are interested in records about their children's progress, but even more interesting in knowing what teachers are going to do about it!

READING SKILLS

The ability to read and write is important for every child and strategies to promote these essentials should figure strongly in your planning and teaching. Without strong reading skills a child is severely disadvantaged, so an important part of your role as a teacher is to help everyone make rapid progress in this area of learning. Reading touches every part of the curriculum and children need to be competent in two ways:

- **The ability to read confidently a book that forms part of a structured reading approach. These books are generally fictional. This aspect is sometimes referred to as *reading for pleasure*.**

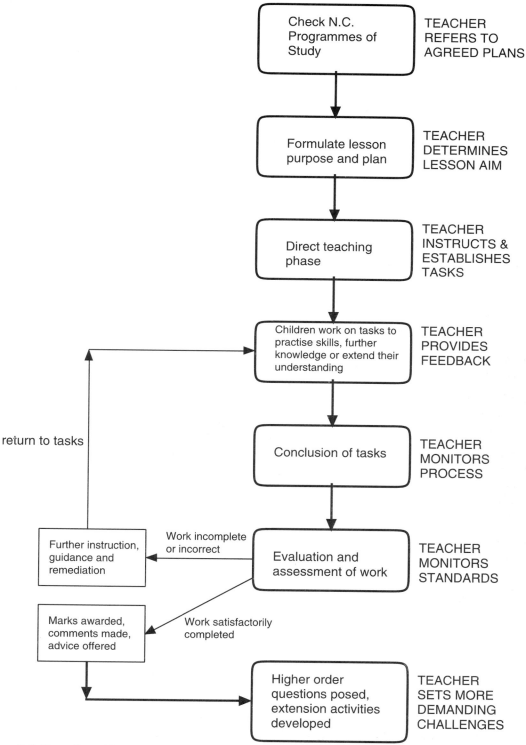

Figure 6.6 Overall teaching process

- **The ability to read, interpret and understand information from non-fiction texts. This is encompassed within the expression *reading for understanding*.**

Most teachers of younger children spend a lot of time developing and broadening children's vocabulary to enable them to enjoy fiction texts. Sometimes a school uses a single reading scheme to support the development of these basic skills; more often teachers use a combination of different reading schemes, in which case books of similar difficulty are colour coded and kept together so that a selection can be made by the teacher or child from within the colour band.

The reading scheme is often closely linked with other aspects of literacy: talking, listening, spelling and writing. The children's early progress in reading is always supported by regular lessons in which word sounds and combinations of sounds are learned and practised (phonics). Most teachers make up word games, and use rhymes, songs and repetition to capture the children's imagination and interest, and reinforce their learning. It is important for children to master the basic elements of phonics and word recognition in *reading for pleasure* before reading for information is tackled seriously. Although examination of non-fiction sources can help to improve children's ability to read, it is unfair to expect them to cope with complex texts without the basic skills to support them in the task.

Reading for information takes many forms, but children are typically asked to find out:

- **as much as possible about a given subject;**
- **the answers to specific questions from a wide range of available books;**
- **answers from a *limited* number of books on a subject, selected in advance by the teacher;**
- **how different books on the same subject present information.**

Later on, children need to master the skill of collecting together a lot of information and extracting key points in a concise form. Do not assume that as long as there is an adequate range of interesting books available, the children will somehow know instinctively how to summarise facts. If you allow children unrestricted use of texts, they will simply end up copying chunks out of them or tracing the pictures into their books.

It is important that children can make judgements about the value of written information (in History, for example). Strategies to evaluate the validity of different written sources and draw conclusions from them demand advanced reading skills and cannot be carried out by less competent readers without adult support.

Words are not confined to books. Other inexpensive and readily available sources such as newspapers, telephone directories, comics, advertisements and catalogues can be utilised to develop simple activities which promote the children's comprehension and enjoyment of reading. For instance, clippings from newspapers can be cut up and glued onto card with interesting questions written below; unusual names can be looked up in directories; children can be asked to make up slogans for advertisements and a short commentary to go with it. The results of these activities can be shared with others in the group or the class, used as a basis for written work, or displayed. There is no limit to the variety of interesting and educational uses for common examples of the printed word.

Monitoring progress in reading

Like every other curriculum activity, reading must be for a purpose. In the earlier stages of reading, you need to monitor closely the children's mistakes and make a note of them for future lessons. In doing so, it is essential to use the class teacher's record system which often consists of a grid onto which exact details of the mistakes are entered. As you become familiar with the range and type of mistakes that are made, you can fit them into your future lesson plans or use odd minutes during the day to rehearse and instruct in them.

Children make many errors in reading: they may not recognise certain words, may mispronounce them, reverse them or not know them. You have to decide whether to correct the error immediately or later. Sometimes, a small error is unimportant in the context of the passage; sometimes it is vital. It is important for you to maintain sensitivity as you seek to help children with their reading, so avoid saying things like: 'No, Jilly! I've told you that word lots of times'. Instead, you need to give Jilly some strategies for recognising the word next time or working out its sound. So it is better to say: 'Let's have another look at that word, shall we?'. Children often correct themselves before you can say anything more. Do not allow wild guesses; rather, tell the child the word and suggest that you read the sentence again together. Monitoring progress in reading demands close attention to individual needs and suitable remedies or extension activities. Reading skills are too important to be left to chance (Clark, 1994).

Hearing readers

Hearing children read aloud is an important element in helping them to develop their reading skills. Most children love to read to an adult or to another child, but you need be aware of the great trust that this requires. Encouragement and sympathetic support is vital if you are to get the best from a child. Take note that more capable readers are actually slowed by reading aloud, so there is little point in doing so other than practising for formal occasions (see later in this section).

It is not enough simply to hear children read as a classroom ritual; you have to decide on its *purpose*. In doing so, it helps to consider that a child reading to the teacher may be useful for one or more of four reasons:

- **It confirms the importance of reading in the mind of the child.**
- **It allows the child to practise alongside an experienced reader (you!)**
- **It gives you opportunity to offer guidance, enthuse about the book's content and note particular errors made by the child.**
- **It offers the child the opportunity to find fulfilment through close interaction with you and success in reading.**

There are a number of different ways of organising readers, including:

- *Individually*
This is logistically difficult if you are responsible for the whole class, unless you give the rest of the children a holding task (such as a simple drawing activity) or have an assistant who can

supervise the other children while you concentrate on the reader. In practice, individual readers can only be heard at times when you can guarantee few or no interruptions, such as breaks or during assembly, or by training an adult volunteer.

■ *Paired reading*

Two children take it in turns to read to one another. The children share books and talk about their content, vocabulary, illustrations and interesting portions of the text (Topping, 1995).

■ *Reading circles*

A reading circle comprises a group of children all using the same book and following the text at the same speed as different children (or the adult) read in turn. If you use reading circles, try to be innovative. For instance, all the children can read together with you in a hushed tone; children can be sub-divided into small groups of two or three and you can call out the name of the sub-group when you want them to read at the same time, ensuring that every child is involved; you can read to the group on the understanding that when you stop, they continue, and when you begin reading again, they stop.

■ **Formal sessions with the whole class**

In this case, the whole class read a series of sentences or a short passage, prepared in advance by you, relating to a specific topic or area of work. The sentences can be written on cards or an overhead projector sheet. As with all whole class work, there are problems of doing something that is appropriate for every ability range. However, used in small amounts, with a fun element attached, the whole class session can be very productive in familiarising all the children with basic vocabulary and key sentences.

Many reading schemes utilise a number of accompanying exercises or tasks to develop different reading skills and concepts, though it is not necessary for you to shoulder the whole responsibility for hearing children read, as classroom assistants, parent volunteers and older children from a different class can be involved. Whatever system is used, your enthusiasm, sense of timing, and love for reading can transform a potentially ordinary session into a dynamic learning opportunity.

Taking books home

There will almost certainly be a system for children to take books home to practise their reading and you need to allow for the time it takes to monitor this procedure. When you encourage a child to take home a particular book, bear in mind that parents may scrutinise it closely. Parental co-operation with the school is an important factor in children's progress. Some schools have an informal pact with parents in which the parents agree to listen regularly to their children reading at home.

Advanced skills

More able readers and older primary children need to be extended in their reading. By introducing more complex words systematically, and talking about colloquialisms, subject specific terminology, catchphrases and the like, you can inspire the children to deepen their understanding and develop new forms of expression, rather than restricting themselves to well-trodden reading paths and failing to extend their vocabulary range. It is worth bearing in mind that children will have to cope with demanding subject texts once they move to secondary school. You will be helping them in this process by concentrating on advanced skills such as skim reading and scanning while they are still in the primary phase.

Public reading

Reading aloud can also be practised through involvement in reading to other members of the class, assembly, and formal public performances in front of parents. Reading in public can be quite traumatic for many children, so thorough preparation is essential. The following guidelines will assist the process of preparing the children:

- **Ensure that the words are clearly written on stiff card.**
- **Give children plenty of time to absorb the sentiments expressed by the words (or the reading will sound empty and meaningless).**
- **Practise with the children over a reasonable period of time, teaching them to read slowly, to lift their heads and voices, and to pause when indicated on the card.**
- **Annotate the readings with words like 'deep breath here' and 'pause for three seconds'. Make sure that the words or sentences are set out in such a clear way that the child can read them with confidence.**

Children gain great pleasure from reading aloud if they feel that they have acquitted themselves well. It can be agony for those who are struggling. Only concentrated, carefully guided practise will ensure that the best is achieved.

Checklist of reading skills

Basic information that *inexperienced* readers need to know includes:

- **A knowledge of the alphabet.**
- **The ability to recognise and name letters.**
- **Familiarity with individual and combination letter sounds in different types of words.**
- **Recognition of key words and groups of words.**

More skilled readers should be able to:

- **use the context of a passage to interpret the text;**
- **predict common patterns of words;**
- **use their knowledge of grammar to clarify meanings.**

This means that you will need to be thoroughly familiar with how to teach phonics, whole word recognition and sentence structure. Your children will progress more quickly in their reading if you encourage them to share books, listen to one another read, and balance a systematic approach to reading with innovative methods.

Reading, writing and topic work

We have seen that using books as sources of information is a skill that requires consistent instruction and guidance. If you have a group who are inexperienced readers, it is helpful to provide a narrow range of reference books, together with some straightforward questions linked directly with particular sections of each book. For instance, you can make cards with the name of a particular book at the top of each card, and provide relevant questions which give the number of the page on which the answer can be found. In this way, children's attention is focused on a relatively small body of text rather than struggling with an index and scanning large chunks of print (Lewis and Wray, 1995). As the children become more experienced and their research skills more refined, the search for information can cover a range of books rather than a single one, using the index.

It is also useful to write out, in advance, key sets of words relating to the topic. These can be written on large sheets for permanent display in the room. The words can be divided into common nouns, proper nouns, adjectives and verbs. For instance, a Science topic on 'Materials and their Properties' with eight year-olds might begin with a list such as:

- *common nouns:* **rock, clay, mineral, hardness, sheen, sharpness, texture, permeability** ...
- *proper nouns:* **Woodbury Common, Fernglade Forest, Meldon Quarry** ...
- *adjectives:* **shiny, flinty, smooth, grainy, darker, speckled, angular** ...
- *verbs:* **strike, cut, handle, compare, describe, classify, measure** ...

As the topic develops, children can add their own words to the list. In this way, a basic vocabulary is available to children, linking reading, writing and knowledge of the subject area.

The *early stages* of writing often involve the child telling the teacher what to write and copying it. Some approaches utilise individual words on cards that can be composed into sentences. Many schools encourage children to try to write for themselves before the teacher gives specific guidance and corrects mistakes. More experienced writers keep their own word books and ask for spellings, but this often produces a queue of children wanting similar words. It is more productive to write the key words in advance on card or the board. As children begin to write for a variety of purposes and audiences, the process tends to follow a pattern. A draft copy is produced, shared with the teacher, corrected and amended, and produced as a final version (see Figure 6.7). Less able children can be encouraged to produce a word processed version on the computer to accompany their hand written effort. The final edition is shared with the audience (the teacher, another adult or child, members of the same group, a younger child in another class, and so on).

Writing is important in every curriculum area. For example, in science experiments, map directions, mathematical investigations, opinions about famous paintings, responses to local environmental issues. More traditional forms such as diaries, letters, re-telling familiar tales and free imaginative (creative) writing also have their place in children's writing experience.

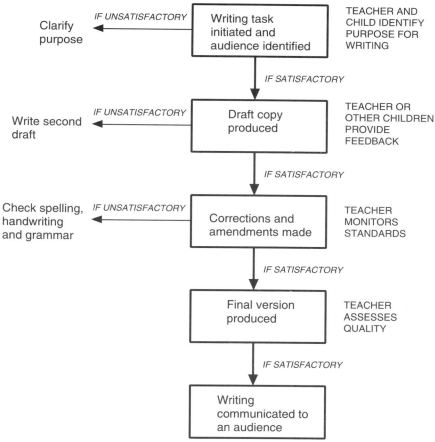

Clarify purpose	← IF UNSATISFACTORY — Writing task initiated and audience identified	TEACHER AND CHILD IDENTIFY PURPOSE FOR WRITING
	↓ IF SATISFACTORY	
Write second draft	← IF UNSATISFACTORY — Draft copy produced	TEACHER OR OTHER CHILDREN PROVIDE FEEDBACK
	↓ IF SATISFACTORY	
Check spelling, handwriting and grammar	← IF UNSATISFACTORY — Corrections and amendments made	TEACHER MONITORS STANDARDS
	↓ IF SATISFACTORY	
	Final version produced	TEACHER ASSESSES QUALITY
	↓ IF SATISFACTORY	
	Writing communicated to an audience	

Figure 6.7 The stages of a writing task

SUPPORT SKILLS

Use of the Overhead Projector

The Overhead Projector (OHP) is extremely useful when you have information for a large group of children (such as a whole class). Amongst other things, OHPs allow you to compile lists, show illustrations and project silhouettes. Like all electrical equipment, the OHP must be treated with care and respect. Although most models are fairly robust, they must be checked regularly by a qualified electrician. To avoid injury to yourself and the machine, a suitable trolley should be used to move the OHP to different locations.

PRACTICALITIES

You need to consider the projector's position in the room in respect of finding a suitable surface as a screen, a safe location and avoiding too much direct light falling on the screen. If you intend to use the OHP as a central part of your teaching in a session, check the focusing beforehand and find out what to do should the bulb fail. Many models have a facility by which you can switch to the back-up bulb by moving a lever at the rear of the machine. It pays to spend a few moments reminding yourself of the practicalities before commencing a lesson.

THE OHP AND PLANNING

Using an OHP does not reduce preparation time. You still need to write out your notes and prepare transparencies for the machine. If you are presenting a large number of facts, the children need to know whether they have to copy anything down or whether you are going to supply a handout. It is important to limit the amount of information on a single transparency sheet, and write in a clear, dark pen. If you have a lot of material use several sheets, numbering them for ease of use. If you have a list of things to show, it is helpful to use a piece of card and gradually reveal each word, sentence or picture in the sequence you have decided.

OTHER USES

The OHP offers possibilities for innovative teaching approaches. Possibilities include:

- **Superimposing several transparency sheets as you build up a composite picture or diagram.**
- **Using a variety of colours to transform a dull set of words into an attractive image.**
- **Highlighting key phrases, phonic parts, and grammatical examples by writing them in a colour which is different from the rest of the script.**
- **Using findings or ideas produced on a transparency by groups of children. You can subsequently show them to the class and discuss the different presentations.**
- **Drawing or photocopying pictures or cartoons (without infringing copyright) as a basis for a story or description of an event.**

An Overhead Projector is a tool. It will not, of itself, improve your teaching. It can, however, enable you to develop a further skill in your portfolio. Always keep a supply of good quality pens safely stored, both washable and permanent.

Mounting a display

Class teachers differ in their opinions about the value of classroom displays. While one will insist on every child contributing something, others will use only commercially produced materials. As you consider your own position, put yourself in the children's place as they survey what has been displayed:

- **What impact does it have on them?**
- **What learning is available through it?**
- **How can it be utilised in your teaching?**
- **What effect does it have upon the children's motivation?**

The visual appearance of displays is important, not merely for enlivening the classroom but for enriching children's learning experiences. During a FASE, it is better to use a small area and display things well than attempt too much. Displays that incorporate some children's work and some of your own special touches, and allow children to touch, handle and engage with the ideas on show, are probably the most effective.

Board writing

Writing clearly and horizontally on the board is an essential skill for teachers. The younger the children, the larger and clearer your printing should be. Joined up writing can be difficult unless the board is in good condition. The only way to improve your board skills is to practise after school. If your writing tends to slope away, take a couple of minutes to draw some parallel, horizontal lines with a pale pen or chalk before the lesson begins. There are many different types of handwriting schemes used by schools, so check the details during your preliminary visit.

Keeping track of things

With so much happening in school, it is easy to get disorganised and overlook important matters. Use of a *Reminders* sheet will help you to keep track of the many demands upon your time. Figure 6.8 is an example of what a completed sheet might look like.

Teaching skills do not improve by magic. It is important that you take time to refine and improve them continually. However, one teaching skill is so important that it has a chapter to itself – *Maintaining Classroom Order*.

	Before school	During school	After school
MONDAY	• cut up paper for art • put up spelling lists • photocopy History worksheets for Tuesday	• break duty with Mr Erickson • check with class teacher about Friday's assembly	• make sure Jessica goes home with dad tonight • check science equipment for tomorrow • mount paintings
TUESDAY	• check small games apparatus • see Mrs Kali about Ben's absence • ask Julie to hear readers	• see class teacher at dinner time for planning • supervisor in to see me teach after break	• Team meeting until 4.30 • Get maths blocks for Wednesday
WEDNESDAY	• check lists of readers • organize instruments for this afternoon	• hall out of action all day • computer club at lunch time	• get marking up to date! • pick up reference books from library
THURSDAY	• confirm new maths groups with Mr Erickson • phone museum centre about exhibition items	• observation in Mr Singh's class this morning • meeting with supervisor at 2 p.m. about my progress	• go with Muriel to pick up exhibition items • cut out plates for tomorrow's technology
FRIDAY	• help class teacher to sort out readings for assembly	• work alongside Mr Singh for technology lesson • observe target child during problem-solving task	• write up case study notes • check software for Monday • fill in profile sheet

Figure 6.8 Reminders

CHAPTER 7

Classroom Order

A teacher should be prepared to give rational explanations for rules which (s)he intends to enforce, and to see that those who are obliged to conform understand them

(Bowley, 1961)

Maintaining order is more a function of good classroom management than of finding a technique to quell rebellious children. There are no easy methods or short cuts to achieving an harmonious classroom environment. If this is your first teaching experience, it is possible that you may not have major responsibility for whole class discipline yet, but you will want to ensure that your work with individuals and small groups is a pleasant and positive time rather than a stressful and traumatic one.

INTERACTING WITH CHILDREN

We have seen that thorough preparation for a teaching experience pays dividends. The sternest test of resolve does not come in the preparation work, however, but through interaction with the children. From the first moment of their contact with children in school, all students have to be alert to their reponsibilities as trainee teachers and the impact they have upon their pupils. Most children are open and straightforward in their relationships with adults. As a newcomer to the classroom, you may be surprised about the things that children ask – 'Who are you?' 'What's your name?' 'Are you a teacher?' 'Are you (the teacher's) wife/husband?' Providing the questions are not asked in a rude or insolent manner, it is best to answer honestly and seriously, pleasantly but not ingratiatingly. Once you have answered, it is reasonable to ask the children some questions in return – 'How long have you been at this school?' 'Do you have any brothers or sisters here?' 'What is your favourite subject?' As children respond, it is essential to maintain good eye contact and appear genuinely

> The term discipline is normally used to describe the effect that the teacher has on classroom order. The term behaviour refers to the child's actions. Classroom order is created by a combination of the two.

interested in what they are saying, as insincerity is soon detected. These brief exchanges are important in establishing a bond with the children in the early days of your teaching experience as you establish your identity.

- **You are not harsh or unreasonable (reasonable is not the same as weak).**
- **You are prepared to be firm, stand no-nonsense and *insist* on good behaviour.**
- **You have the tenacity to cope with the situation.**
- **You are an interesting person who will teach interesting lessons.**
- **You are fair in your dealings with children.**

It is natural for children of all ages to want to find out where you draw the line in the things you are prepared to accept and allow. They want to discover something of your character and (in a few cases) exploit your weaknesses. The older the children, the more thorough this searching will be, so in the early days of your school experience it is important for you to:

- **say what you mean and mean what you say;**
- **avoid creating problems due to your own negligence;**
- **resisting blaming the children as a result of your own failings or anxieties.**

Your character is an important factor in gaining the children's respect, in particular the degree of *sparkle* you possess, as demonstrated through:

- **strong eye contact;**
- **helpful and prompt responses to children's questions;**
- **varying your tone, pitch and pace;**
- **a lively, consistent teaching approach.**

You will meet many different kinds of children in any school. Some cling to you like leeches and seek constant reassurance. Others are bossy and noisy and challenging. Yet others are as timid as mice. And here they come into your classroom! Taking a positive attitude to discipline is vital (see figure 7.1). Children despise students who let them get away with being rude and naughty, who are over-familiar or who patronise them. Worse, children hate students who try to humiliate them, use harsh control methods and show blatant favouritism.

On the other hand, children like students to allow them the time and opportunity to express their own interests and feelings. They warm to students who appreciate them as individuals and demonstrate this by showing a mixture of kindness, sensitivity and a willingness to show understanding and firmness in equal measure.

As a trainee teacher, you need to create the right impression with the children and with the class teacher through

- **your appearance**
- **enthusiasm and inspiration**
- **conscientiousness**
- **maturity (this is teaching, not a holiday camp)**
- **thorough lesson preparation**

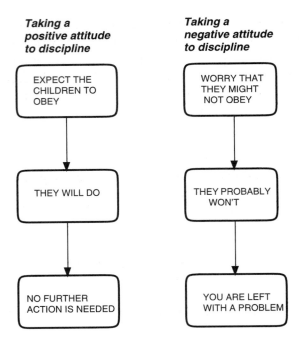

Figure 7.1 Discipline expectations

- application to the task
- attention to detail
- good humour (but not ridiculously so)
- maintaining a sense of proportion about classroom events.

Children have contact with adults every day and always respond positively to those teachers and students who themselves have a positive attitude to learning.

KEEPING THINGS IN PERSPECTIVE

No teacher or child is perfect. Despite all your efforts to keep classroom events under control, there are bound to be times when things go wrong. It takes time to get to know a class, and during the settling in period misunderstandings and uncomfortable moments are almost inevitable as the necessary adjustments take place. When you know that what you are doing is right, it essential that you persevere and do not allow yourself to be diverted from the path that you have chosen. This is different from being rigid and blinkered in your view. We have seen that flexibility in teaching is important, but if the children are testing your patience through silliness or lack of respect, you must hold unswervingly to your principles and insist on their compliance. You will not do any favours to yourself or the children by hesitating when you need to be determined. If you are unsure of the reason for children's behaviour patterns, and cannot resolve them by talking to the children about them, always gain advice from the class teacher or supervisor. Do not flounder on until your confidence has sapped away or the children are making your life a misery.

On the other hand, do not fall into the trap of assuming that the inappropriate things children do are deliberately aimed at creating disturbance or mischief. When a student is uneasy about how to cope with a group of children, it is common for the student to accuse, sound suspicious or express open dismay about the actions of children. This attitude is often counter-productive as it creates an unpleasant atmosphere and can cause resentment. Compare these alternative scenarios:

Accusations

■ **In response to a child who has used the wrong colour of paper for an activity, assuming that the child is acting *wilfully* ...**

STUDENT 1: Charlie! Why don't you do as you are told like everybody else? I'm fed up with you spoiling things.

CHARLIE: Jenny told me to ...

STUDENT 1: I don't care what Jenny said. I'm fed up with you. You never seem to get things right because you don't bother to listen!

Contrast this with a response which assumes that *misunderstanding* rather than mischief is the cause:

STUDENT 2: Charlie. Why are you using the green paper?

CHARLIE: I thought we were supposed to. Jenny said.

STUDENT 2: No. I said to use blue. Could you put that sheet back, please, and use the proper colour. And make sure that Jenny knows as well. Thank you.

Sounding suspicious

■ **In response to a child who comes in late from playtime ...**

STUDENT 1: Shelley, why are you late for class?

SHELLEY: Miss, 'cause I had to get my lunch box ...

STUDENT 1: Not that lunch box again! I told you to leave it inside the classroom. If you're late again because of your lunch box, I'll keep you inside during playtimes.

Contrasting with the student who waits until the explanation is complete:

STUDENT 2: Shelley, why are you late for class?

SHELLEY: Miss, 'cause I had to get me lunch box. Me mum forgot to give it me this morning, so she brought it at playtime and I had to get it from Mr Sale's office and he was busy, Miss, and he said that I was to say sorry for the delay, Miss.

STUDENT 2: Alright, Shelley. Thank you for telling me. Put your box in the corner and I'll explain to you what we're doing during this lesson.

Expressing dismay

■ **In response to a child who hands in a story written in very poor handwriting ...**

STUDENT 1: Lin, this is awful. I'm not accepting a piece of work looking like that. Go away and write it neatly.

LIN: But Sir, I can't do it any better . . .

STUDENT 1:   If I tell you to do it better, you'll do it better, or I'll see you after the lesson and give you extra handwriting practice!

As opposed to the student who does not jump to conclusions:

STUDENT 2:   Lin, this is awful. I'm not accepting a piece of work looking like that. Go away and write it neatly.

LIN: But Sir, I can't do it any better. I fell off the swing last night and hurt my wrist and so I'm using my left hand, Sir, and it keeps wobbling about when I write, Sir.

STUDENT 2:   Oh, I'm sorry to hear that, Lin. I wish you had told me earlier. You could have used the computer to write your story instead.

These examples show that with a little patience and understanding, the first student could have avoided upsetting the child and improved the climate of trust and confidence. The second student took a more positive view and listened carefully to the child's explanation before assuming the worst. It does not take a lot of imagination to guess which student will eventually have the happiest and most loyal class of children.

Taking this positive view does not mean being gullible. Children sometimes behave badly by choice or deliberately spoil things, but these instances are relatively rare. However, a positive classroom climate does not happen by chance, so you need to persevere and set an example to the children through your own attitude and behaviour. It pays to spend a little time reflecting on how you respond to children's behaviour. Knowing yourself will help to keep things in perspective.

Class mood

It is also important to be sensitive to subtle changes in class mood. For instance, if you insist on pressing forward with a teaching approach when the children are clearly restless and agitated, it is inevitable that the situation will deteriorate. Instead, try a change of direction (such as giving a relatively straightforward task that keeps the class occupied and seated, or bringing the class together on the carpet for a story, or giving an open-ended task for a short time) until the children are more settled.

Although you need to ensure that children do not deliberately avoid the set work by their lack of co-operation, it is important not to spend too long in one mode of teaching (such as whole class teaching or collaborative problem solving) if by doing so you invite boredom. Remember that small children can only concentrate on the same task for a short time, and there is also a limit to the time a child can spend on desk-bound tasks which require hard thinking. More restful, creative activities are not only useful in their own right, but provide essential contrasts within a child's learning programme. If you can develop a flexibility of approach to accommodate the changing class mood, you will have added an important feature to your armoury of strategies for maintaining control and enhancing the classroom ethos.

Negative attitudes

When you have to insist that children do work that they find difficult or tedious, your own enthusiasm and ability to encourage the children will make a considerable difference to their attitude. It is important to avoid giving the following impressions.

IT MAY BE BORING BUT IT WILL DO YOU GOOD

This can be transmitted to the children through adopting a lacklustre approach, uninspiring teaching methods (such as when you do far too much talking) or failing to explain the relevance of a lesson and just letting them loose on a perplexing task.

YOU HAVE JUST GOT TO PUT UP WITH IT

This is transmitted through maintaining a rigid outlook (such as being unwilling to listen to children's ideas and suggestions), gritting your teeth and finishing a teaching episode even if it is quite obvious that it isn't working, becoming harsh or dismissive with children who complain about the irrelevance or inappropriateness of a lesson rather than discussing alternative approaches.

THE MOST IMPORTANT THING IS TO PLEASE THE TEACHER

This is transmitted through stifling creativity, scorning unsatisfactory work and praising too highly those children who produce conformist work; restricting opportunities for children to share with one another; only using approving comments about the visible outcome of work and not the effort made in producing it.

ONE TYPE OF BEHAVIOUR IS FAVOURED UNDULY

This is transmitted through consistently praising particular answers and criticising others; publicly humiliating a child through sarcasm or scorn; showing a clear preference for one type of child (usually the co-operative, passive ones) and failing to acknowledge improvement in the behaviour of less conformist children.

Children soon become aware of a teacher's attitude towards work: enthusiasm, tolerance, comments, reactions. They note the teacher's propensity to favour one circumstance above others. They become alert to a teacher's tendency to approve of one child and scorn another. If you take a positive attitude to teaching and learning rather than a negative one, it will pay dividends in the quality of the children's reactions and behaviour.

Rules

Lots of classes and schools have a set of agreed rules. These are sometimes so broad that they are meaningless, and sometimes so precise that the children would have to be saints to remain within the boundaries. As a student teacher you are not in a position to challenge or neglect the classroom or school rules, but it pays to be aware that most sets of rules need to be interpreted realistically. Two common examples help to demonstrate the issue.

ASK PERMISSION BEFORE YOU TOUCH OTHER CHILDREN OR THEIR POSSESSIONS

Violations of this often occur due to sheer enthusiasm at the sight of (say) another child's new toy, or friendly, clumsy gestures from (say) a lonely child. The spirit of the rule is sensible as a means of protecting vulnerable children, minimising theft and detering bullying, but there are many occasions when touch is spontaneous and generous. It would be ridiculous, for instance, to rebuke two five year-olds for holding hands in the playground.

WALK IN THE CLASSROOM AND CORRIDORS

This is a sensible rule, but there are times when children skip, hop and run in their eagerness to complete a task and gain your approval. A gentle reminder is often appropriate, delivered in the context of wanting to protect the children from harm.

Two principles emerge from these examples:

- **Take account of motives when applying the rule.**
- **If a rule is infringed due to forgetfulness or over-enthusiasm, reprimands should normally take the form of gentle reminders rather than harsh comments. Insolent or deliberate behaviour is a different matter (see below).**

CLASSROOM DISORDER

Classroom disorder does not happen by chance. Sometimes, your inexperience helps to create problems where it might have been avoided. On other occasions, a situation (such as intense excitement at Christmas) makes life difficult for even the most experienced teacher.

There is nothing worse than having to spend a lot of your time dealing with incidents resulting from poor behaviour and feeling that you may be about to lose control of the teaching situation. Nearly all students suffer from nerves, especially when left alone with the whole class, so do not think that you are a failure if, at times, it seems that things are on the point of disintegrating. In fact, you are probably doing far better than you realise. All students (and teachers) have their ups-and-downs in maintaining a healthy, effective classroom environment and it is very rare for a situation to get completely out of control. Take advice from experienced teachers about control strategies, but remember that imitating their methods is no guarantee of success.

There is no such thing as a typical class of children. However, you can be certain that there will always be at least one child who causes you concern. Sometimes the child deliberately tests you through their behaviour; more often their natural attitude and actions annoy you. If a child is challenging your authority, you can either ignore it and try to continue regardless, or resist it. If you ignore the behaviour, there is a small chance that the child will tire of it and begin to conform. However, it is more likely that matters will deteriorate. You have to learn to evaluate the situation quickly and decide whether:

a) the child is unaware of how much the behaviour is annoying you;
b) the child is normally sensible but is being silly on this occasion;
c) the child is mischievous and has found a way of exploiting a situation;
d) the child is wilfully opposing you.

As you get to know the children, your judgement will become more accurate. The first three options are common; the last one is rare. A useful strategy is to assume that a) is operating before b) before c) before d). That is, respond initially by assuming option a) is happening. For example:

'Peter, no-one can hear when you tap your ruler on the table all the time. Please put it down and leave it alone'. (And when he obeys): *'Thank you'.*

If, by the expression on Peter's face and his general body language, you know that he is being silly, you might then respond using option b):

'Peter, if you tap the ruler on the table, it will damage it, and I will be very upset with you. Please stop it right now and pay attention to me.'

If the behaviour continues, a stronger response is required and option c) is clearly relevant:

'Peter, please bring the ruler to me at playtime after everyone else has gone out to play and I'll decide whether or not to take you to . . .' (the adult he most fears). Then carry on immediately with the lesson. If Peter continues to mess with the ruler, he is being deliberately provocative (option d) and must be dealt with firmly. Even if he protests loudly, take him (do not send him or send a child to accompany him) to the class teacher. If this is not possible or Peter resists, send a couple of reliable children to fetch the class teacher or the nearest adult.

Extreme measures are not normally necessary if you have taken the advice offered in this chapter, but occasionally a child has such severe emotional and behavioural problems that decisive action is needed. You may find that there is an opportunity to speak calmly to Peter when the situation has eased; if so, it is worth re-establishing your relationship with him as soon as possible. If Peter is capable of defying you, there is a strong likelihood that he has behaved in a similar way before and is known to the senior staff of the school. Do not expect Peter to conform simply because you were firm on one occasion. Once children have exhibited the sort of wilful behaviour described above, you will have to persist in setting them short-term achievable goals and enforce rigidly the limits of their conduct. Children with severe behavioural problems sometimes have an additional classroom helper allocated to them. Work closely with the helper and the class teacher, and log serious infringements of the rules.

Avoiding unnecessary difficulties

No matter how much you excel as a classroom practitioner, you will inevitably encounter circumstances which test your resolve and your ability to nurture a pleasant, hard-working atmosphere. It is essential that you do not see the situation as an us-and-them conflict. By following these guidelines, you will make your task easier.

MAKE IT CLEAR WHAT YOU EXPECT

If you do not make your expectations explicit, do not be surprised if the children make their own decisions. It is not fair to rebuke a child for showing some initiative and doing the wrong thing if it resulted from your poor initial explanation.

DO NOT DISTRACT THE CHILDREN UNNECESSARILY

If children are working sensibly, minimise any comments which might cause them to lose their train of thought or offer opportunity for disruption. For instance, if you comment in the middle of the lesson that: 'We need to get a move on; there's a play rehearsal after this', you should not be surprised if the calm atmosphere is replaced by merriment, excited questions and animated conversations. It may take several minutes to retrieve such a situation.

On the other hand, *building in pauses* in an otherwise intensive lesson serves an important function. These pauses are different from incidental distractions. They can be written into your lesson plans as discrete episodes. For instance:

> *Recapping the lesson's purpose*
> Thus: 'Stop for a moment and look this way. I can see that you are making some impressive looking hexagons, but different people have got different numbers of lines of symmetry, so please check to make sure that you haven't missed any. Right, carry on.'
>
> *Approving good practice*
> 'Look up for a moment and see how well Mushtaq has used different shades of blue and grey for the sky . . .'
>
> *Reminding the class of procedures*
> 'I'm pleased with your hand writing but I notice that some people are using a small version of the capital J in the middle of a word rather than the small case letter. Watch carefully while I demonstrate the correct method.'

GIVE INSTRUCTIONS IN THE ORDER THEY SHOULD TAKE PLACE

Do not say: 'You can all go out to play when you finish tidying up' but rather: 'Once you have finished tidying up, you can go out to play'. If you use the former statement, it is likely that you will have to stop some children who already are flying towards the door! The order of words in the second option makes it clear that the right to go out to play is dependent upon completing the tidying. If this is your intention, do not allow anyone to go until you are satisfied with their efforts.

DON'T USE WORDS AS A WEAPON

Words are like toothpaste; once they are squeezed out, they can never be taken back. It is possible for you to reinforce unhelpful stereotypes by your choice of words and associated body language. For example, if you always sigh and raise your eyebrows when you answer a particular child's question, the child (as well as the other class members) will gradually perceive that you find the child irritating. If you only praise the children who normally do badly, the consistently reliable children may perceive that their conscientiousness does not pay. If you only praise the children who normally do well, the less able children will become dispirited. If you invest in sarcasm as a tool, you could end up bankrupt. Keep your words under control and emphasise your pleasure with children who are obviously doing their very best to succeed in their work and behaviour (Robertson, 1989).

AVOID QUEUES

If you sit at your desk in the classroom and expect children to come to see you when they have a problem, you can guarantee that queues will build up. As you deal with the child at the head of the queue, those behind will push, interfere with nearby tables and become noisy. Some children are expert at waiting in a queue until they are nearly at the front and then suddenly remembering something they have forgotten to do, move out of the line to do it, and rejoin the line at the back. In this way, they avoid work, have lots of fun messing with their friends and causing disruption. Queues are also inefficient as children with trivial questions requiring a brief response are mixed with those who need a lot of your time. For children to wait five minutes in a queue to ask you whether they should write the date on the left or right hand side of the page is ridiculous.

Even if you are circulating around the room, helping, checking and assessing work, it is possible to gather a knot of children who follow you about like chicks after a hen. To avoid this situation, make it clear that children who need help should wait until you are available. Make sure you strictly enforce this, or assertive children will claim an undue proportion of your attention. Be careful, too, that you do not keep children waiting for too long or they will spend much of the lesson doing nothing.

If, while circulating, you find that there are a number of similar questions about the work, it is better to stop the group or class and explain to everyone at the same time, rather than endlessly repeating yourself to individual children. Time spent at the start of a session in explaining the work clearly, providing the necessary resources and stating what you expect from the children, will eliminate many of the problems described above.

Miss, she's making me laugh

Children love to have some fun. Sometimes, it is innocent but disruptive. Typical of this is the instance when two friends are sitting together and giggling. This may take place during a time when you are addressing the class or when the children are meant to be working together. For instance:

> 'Miss, she's making me laugh.'
> 'No, I'm not!'
> 'Yes you are; I'm trying to get on with me work and you're stopping me!'
> 'I'm not. I'm not, Miss . . .'

In this brief exchange, it is likely that many other children will be alert to the possibility of some fun and anticipating a welcome breather from their work. Some children will be looking at you, wondering what action you will take. It is likely that one or two will try to assist you by making their own comments: 'They're always mucking about, Miss' or 'Shall I tell (the class teacher) Miss?' or starting their own bit of fun. It may be necessary to deal with these other children first and tell them to get on with their own work. Depending on the circumstances, an effective response from you will draw on one of the following strategies:

A LIGHT TOUCH

If the incident is trivial, use a light touch and avoid disrupting the atmosphere unduly. (Smiling sweetly) 'It's nice to see you both enjoying yourselves in my lesson. Tell me all about it after the *end* of the lesson when you have finished your work'. In most cases this does the trick, and the children will settle down. After a few moments, make sure that you look to see how they are faring.

DEALING WITH DISRUPTORS

If you are aware that the first child is genuinely trying to work, look disapprovingly at the second child without saying anything. If the child does not catch your gaze, keep looking steadfastly unless she looks up. Do not say anything, then signal to the child that she is to come to you. Keep looking with a stern face at the child as she makes her way towards you. Bend forward and say quietly but audibly something like: 'Gemma. If you don't settle down and finish your work and leave Rita alone, you and I will fall out. Is that clear? Is there anything that you don't understand?' It is likely that the class will have fallen silent so that they can hear what you are saying! Once Gemma has acknowledged your warning and responded to your question, allow her to return to her seat, keeping your eyes on her until she has recommenced her work. (It is probable that the two girls will exchange looks and may let a tiny giggle slip, but this is best ignored.)

USE OF UNDERTONES

If both girls seem to be at fault, use a gentle tone with an undertone of something worse to come if they do not comply: 'I'll come over and see who has done most work in one minute's time'. Quite often, one of the girls will come out to see you within the next minute to ask your advice about her work and gain your favour. Usually, the second child will follow soon afterwards. Do not be duped into believing that they have suddenly transformed into hard workers; the behaviour of both girls will still require monitoring.

WARNING REMARKS

If the two children enjoy sitting together, and are clearly messing about, you can use a final warning remark such as: 'It looks as if I may have to find a different partner for both of you next lesson'. If they are anxious to stay together, they will normally settle to work. It may be necessary to separate them in future lessons should the poor application to work continue, though separation is not a long-term solution for children who are bored or disengaged with the task.

What do I do if . . .?

CHILDREN WON'T SETTLE DOWN WHEN I'M TRYING TO TALK TO THE WHOLE CLASS

Continue talking for a time with your eyes firmly set on the malcontents. Do not disrupt the flow of the lesson if possible. If the children continue being inattentive, drop your voice (do not raise it) and make it more difficult for everyone to hear. Quite often, this will cause the inattentive children's attention to be caught and they will stop their silliness. Sometimes, another child in the group will tell them to shush; if so, thank the child and ask one of the distracted children to repeat what you have just said. It is unlikely that the child will be able to, in which case you can quietly but firmly ask one of them to move to another position or inform them that you will be asking them some questions about the work in a moment or two. This usually causes them to pay attention. If you perceive that the children are squirming around because you have spent too long on a formal teaching approach, change direction as soon as possible.

CHILDREN WON'T SETTLE AFTER I'VE ALLOCATED THE TASK

There is always a reason for children's inactivity. Figure 7.2 can be used as a checklist to identify the possible reasons contributing to the behaviours.

I HAVE A GROUP DOING A PRACTICAL EXERCISE AND ONE CHILD IS SNATCHING ALL THE BEST EQUIPMENT

This is a case where prevention is better than cure. The child may be acting selfishly or simply enthusiastically. It is quite common for younger children to go through a stage of feeling envious towards anyone who seems to have more than them. Through clarifying

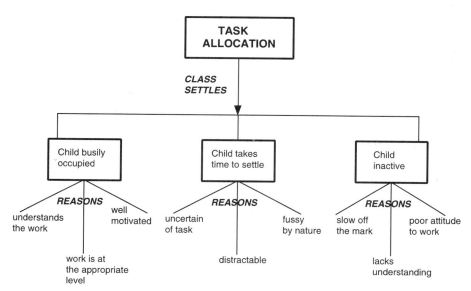

Figure 7.2 Explanations for children's differing attitudes to the task

the procedures and giving a careful, patient explanation, you will gradually redress the imbalance of provision across the group. You may want to consider giving priority to the less assertive children in a future session to ensure that they have a fair chance to use the equipment. Dealing with Devlin who, in response to your encouragement to share, protests desperately: 'Yes, but I need it!' requires great patience and firmness, while reassuring Devlin that he will get his turn; but that others are entitled to their fair share too.

I AM HELPING CHILDREN AT ONE TABLE AND A CHILD FROM ANOTHER TABLE COMES TO TELL ME THAT SOMEONE IS NOT DOING HIS WORK

The way in which you treat informants gives a powerful signal to other children about how they should behave. On the one hand, you do not want to discourage informants; on the other hand, you do not want to encourage gossip or tell-tales. In this example, it is usually best to thank Jessica for telling you and ask her to sit down again. Do not respond immediately, but first complete what you are doing, then go across casually and look to see what is happening. You may find that the child accused (probably correctly) of not working will, on the assumption that attack is the best form of defence, accuse Jessica of doing something wrong as soon as you arrive (if not before). If you concentrate on the *work* with the group of children, rather than their behaviour, it depersonalises the issue and enables you to give direction and advice. Do everything you can to avoid a time of accusation and counter-accusation. It can be very effective to insist: 'Thank you, but if you have anything more to say, please tell me *after* the lesson'.

I AM CLEARING UP AT THE END OF A LESSON AND TWO OR THREE CHILDREN ARE NOT BOTHERING TO HELP

Direct your attention to the lazy children. Tell them that you have noticed their slackness and how tempted you feel to make them do all the tidying up next time while the rest of the class watch. Set them a task, such as bringing you (say) five items that they are putting away, or ten pieces of paper they have picked up off the floor. Some children love to clear up and will happily spend extra time doing so. While you do not want to discourage them, it is important to involve every child in the task.

A CHILD IS DELIBERATELY CASUAL WITH HIS WORK

As you get to know the class better and examine their previous work, your assessment of their ability will become clearer. If Randolph seems indifferent to your insistence upon everyone doing their very best, you can use examples of his previous work to remind him that he is capable of achieving a higher standard. If he claims that he is not working to capacity because he is bored, you are entitled to sound a little exasperated (though perhaps you want to take careful note of what he is saying). Depending on Randolph's age and attitude, there are a number of options:

- **sternly tell him that whether or not he is bored, you expect to see him make his very best effort;**

- **tell him that when he completes a piece of work from now on, you will ask him to grade it himself in addition to receiving your grade;**
- **collect in all his work at the end of the week and spend some time evaluating it with him.**

As a rule, most children are realistic about the quality of their work and effort. It is hard to motivate children who resist all your efforts to involve them in interesting tasks; they sometimes try to negotiate a position by saying, in effect: 'I'll complete the things I like doing with minimum fuss if you don't demand too much of me'. Sadly, for devious children, this is sometimes the best you can hope for.

A GROUP ENGAGED IN A COLLABORATIVE EXERCISE ALLOW THEIR VOICES TO GET TOO LOUD

If the noise is due to over-enthusiasm, try a pleasant remark such as : 'I'm pleased to see you so involved in your work, but the lady in the house across the road can't hear her television because of the racket!' By using this light touch, most children will make the effort to reduce the noise. A simple strategy such as: 'If you think that the noise in the group is getting too much, please start whispering' can also be effective. If the noise is due to lack of engagement with the task, you should provide them with a fresh short term objective to achieve. Whatever the situation, avoid constantly shushing and moaning about the general noise level.

CHILDREN SING ROWDILY DURING A MUSIC LESSON

Children should be taught to sing. If they sing rowdily, it probably means that you have not spent enough time teaching them correctly. Perhaps you should!

Rewards and punishments

Class teachers have their own ideas about the administering of appropriate rewards and punishments, and you will need to conform as closely as possible to them. Some teachers do not like the use of the term *punishment* because of the harshness it conveys, preferring terms such as *sanctions* or *penalties*. A few teachers also object on principle to the use of rewards, arguing that they are artificial and that children become obsessed with receiving them rather than working for the satisfaction of doing well.

In an ideal world, punishments would be unnecessary because children would always conform to expectations. In practice, there are some occasions when a child deliberately flouts the rules and you are faced with deciding upon a suitable sanction. Some interesting work by Harrop and Holmes (1993) indicates that teachers and children sometimes have different views about the effectiveness of punishments. It is worth looking at a few of their findings.

Harrop and Holmes found that whereas telling off children in front of the class or privately was considered to be an effective method by teachers, children were less impressed. Instead, stopping a child from going on a trip was seen by the children as one of the most effective methods, but it was not ranked highly by teachers. Both children and teachers believed that informing parents was the harshest sanction available.

Similarly, teachers and pupils' ideas about the *effectiveness of rewards* differed. Teachers considered that public praise and giving housepoints (or similar) was effective, but these methods were not ranked highly by pupils. Instead, the children considered that parents being informed and getting a good mark for work were the top rewards. Both teachers and children agreed that receiving good written comments on work was important. There are significant points to note from this research:

- **the place of parental approval and disapproval**
- **the importance of written comments**
- **the relevance of verbal comments.**

It is not permissible to use any physical contact to get your way unless a child is in danger. Hitting children is not allowed, so don't countenance doing it, even in fun. Some schools also have policies about touching children, so check that you know what they are.

Rewards and sanctions need to be seen in terms of your wider responsibility as a teacher for developing interesting and relevant lessons. Children are not fooled, and even if you give sparkling rewards and glowing comments about mediocre work, the impact upon their effort or attitude will be minimal. On the other hand, your enthusiastic reactions when children do their best or produce a good piece of work is the motivation that most children seek and need.

An orderly classroom is beneficial both to children and teachers. Children who can work in a calm, purposeful environment are likely to achieve higher standards. You will be able to enjoy the job and give of your best without struggling to maintain order. Good classroom order is not automatic; it requires effort and perseverance. Make it a top priority.

CHAPTER 8

Achieving Competence

> *Professional competences ... define the subject knowledge, teaching skills and personal qualities which all newly qualified primary teachers will be expected to have developed*
>
> *(Circular, 14/93)*

Over the past twenty years, governments have taken an increasingly close interest in the quality of initial teacher training and the continuing professional development of qualified teachers. In 1992 and 1993, two important documents, Circular 9/92 (secondary) and Circular 14/93 (primary) were issued by the Department for Education, DfE (now known as the Department for Education and Employment, DfEE) containing lists of the criteria to be satisfied before awarding qualified teacher status (QTS).

On the basis of some key texts (Alexander et al, 1992; Ofsted, 1993; NCC, 1993), together with information from school inspections, three aspects of primary teaching in which all primary teachers needed to be confident were identified:

1) The subject knowledge needed for primary teaching
2) Choosing and using a range of teaching methods
3) Competence in testing and assessing pupils' progress

In particular, special mention was made of *five aspects of initial training*:

1) Knowledge of, and skills in, teaching the core subjects
2) The basic skills of reading and arithmetic
3) Testing, assessment, recording and reporting
4) The use of individual, group and whole-class methods
5) The ability to maintain order and discipline

The competences contained in the Circular are comprehensive and lengthy. They are based on the premise that no degree or qualification leading to QTS should be awarded unless the student has demonstrated *in the classroom* the ability to teach effectively and to secure effective learning; maintain discipline and manage pupil behaviour.

More recently, the Teacher Training Agency (TTA) made proposals about a national curriculum for use in training teachers (TTA, 1997), in which they stressed the importance of:

1) subject knowledge and understanding
2) planning, teaching and class management
3) monitoring, assessment, recording, reporting and accountability
4) other professional requirements

The TTA proposals emphasise the importance of newly qualified teachers (NQTs) having high expectations of their pupils, and fostering their enthusiasm and motivation. In addition, NQTs must be familiar with the Special Educational Needs Code of Practice (DfE/Welsh Office, 1994), and have a sound knowledge of Information Technology. Primary teachers will, in future, be expected to have strong subject knowledge and teaching ability in English and Mathematics; secondary teachers will need to have acquired a thorough understanding of their specialist subjects and the associated concepts and skills, to degree level standard.

Profiling and the Career Entry Profile

As a response to these demands, all colleges have developed procedures for monitoring students' competence across their training course through *profiles*, which are a systematic method by which both students and tutors can contribute towards building a clear picture of teaching strengths and areas for development. As a student, you will be asked to contribute to your profile, drawing on all aspects of your course, but particularly school experience where you can demonstrate your competence in action. The final stage in profiling is the Career Entry Profile (CEP), a comprehensive documenting of your competence in the five aspects of training noted above. Naturally, your own single subject should be an area of strength, together with a thorough grasp of the core subjects. However, you need to be sufficiently competent in every National Curriculum area before you can receive your QTS. It is essential that you take profiling seriously as it can affect your job prospects and will help towards your development as a teacher, once qualified.

At first sight, the list of competences is daunting and you may wonder if it is possible for anyone to achieve everything that is listed! It is important to remember that the ultimate proof of your abilities as a teacher is seen in whether or not the children are learning effectively. Providing there is evidence to support this fact, most of the other competences are assumed to be satisfactory.

CHECKLIST OF COMPETENCES

The following list of competence statements are based on the DfE 14/93 teaching competences and TTA proposals. For the full text, you should refer to the documents. A

Key Issue is suggested for each statement, and recommendations about the things you need to learn before you can successfully fulfil the criteria in your classroom teaching and staff membership.

Your knowledge and understanding of subjects

YOU WILL NEED TO LEARN ABOUT

- the content of core and foundation subjects, and RE
- the place of subjects as part of pupils' entitlement

YOU WILL NEED TO LEARN ABOUT

- lesson planning in respect of learning intentions and predicted outcomes.
- the relationship between lesson planning and continuity of learning experiences
- the links between lesson purpose, activities and assessment
- coping with subject-related questions

Assessment, recording and reporting (AR & R) of pupils' progress

YOU WILL NEED TO LEARN ABOUT

- pupils' mistakes and misunderstandings
- different types of assessment and their functions
- monitoring and evaluating pupils' progress
- the links between assessment and record-keeping

YOU WILL NEED TO LEARN ABOUT

- the link between lesson planning and assessment
- the way in which these links relate to different subjects and curriculum areas
- progression in learning

Demonstrate your knowledge and understanding of the subjects of the primary curriculum. KEY ISSUE: Subject expertise.

Use that subject knowledge and understanding to plan lessons, teach and assess pupils . KEY ISSUE: Teaching-and-learning single subjects.

By using your assessments of children's progress, judge the standard they have reached with reference to the national requirements. KEY ISSUE: The use of formative, diagnostic (evaluative) and summative forms of assessment.

Use your assessments to guide future planning and teaching. KEY ISSUE: How assessment informs planning

Mark and monitor pupils' progress and provide oral and written feedback to them to help ensure that they have completed and understood the work. KEY ISSUE: Feedback to enhance learning.

Preparing reports for parents
KEY ISSUE: Parent entitlement

YOU WILL NEED TO LEARN ABOUT

- clarifying acceptable standards of achievement
- the importance of providing helpful feedback
- types of feedback appropriate to different circumstances

YOU WILL NEED TO LEARN ABOUT

- differing styles of reports (formal and informal; oral and written)
- appropriate language and terminology to use in reports

Identify clear and appropriate teaching intentions.
KEY ISSUE: Objectives and content.

Understand how pupils learn and of contributing factors that influence learning.
KEY ISSUE: The links between theory and practice.

Effective learning

YOU WILL NEED TO LEARN ABOUT

- theories that help to explain patterns of learning
- the range and signifiacnce of factors that influence the learning process
- the influence of the classroom context upon learning

Take note of individual differences in your planning and teaching.
KEY ISSUE: Relevance for learning.

YOU WILL NEED TO LEARN ABOUT

- learning goals associated with the National Curriculum Programmes of Study
- learning goals not explicitly stated in the National Curriculum
- methods to determine the extent to which learning outcomes are achieved

YOU WILL NEED TO LEARN ABOUT

- the variation in individual differences
- the range of special educational needs
- promoting spiritual, moral, personal, social and cultural education

Set high and relevant expectations for all pupils.
KEY ISSUE: Fulfilling potential.

YOU WILL NEED TO LEARN ABOUT

- the relationship between expectation and outcome in learning
- strategies that can be used for evaluating a pupil's potential
- ways to enrich and extend children's learning

Teaching strategies and techniques

YOU WILL NEED TO LEARN ABOUT

- responding with interest to the things children say
- developing both closed and open-ended questions
- the skills required for instructing and explaining

Communicating effectively with pupils.
KEY ISSUE: Genuine interaction.

YOU WILL NEED TO LEARN ABOUT

- time allocation to different areas of the curriculum
- your own time management inside and outside the classroom
- strategies for helping pupils to make the best use of their time
- the dangers of frittering away valuable time in pointless activities

Effective time management.
KEY ISSUE: Efficiency.

Help pupils to develop individual and collaborative study skills.
KEY ISSUE: Learning together.

YOU WILL NEED TO LEARN ABOUT

- number and literacy skills that are useful across the curriculum
- study skills that facilitate enquiry, recording of results and talking about findings

YOU WILL NEED TO LEARN ABOUT

- different models of classroom control.
- factors which contribute towards a purposeful, orderly and supportive environment.
- the importance of clarifying tasks and procedures.
- the need to offer pupils strategies for them to develop self control

Establishing good and appropriate standards of classroom discipline.
KEY ISSUE: Orderly yet purposeful.

YOU WILL NEED TO LEARN ABOUT

- stimulating pupils' interest
- imaginative teaching approaches.
- strategies for establishing high quality teacher-pupil interaction.
- techniques for introducing lessons and tasks clearly and concisely.

Using a variety of whole class, group and individual teaching approaches.
KEY ISSUE: Flexibility of approach.

Establishing and maintaining a purposeful teaching environment.
KEY ISSUE: Creative teaching.

Utilising information technology. KEY ISSUE: Technological support for learning.

YOU WILL NEED TO LEARN ABOUT

- methods of organizing for learning
- examples of one-to-one, group and whole class teaching strategies
- different teaching techniques and their appropriateness
- employing a range of techniques across a given teaching session

YOU WILL NEED TO LEARN ABOUT

- computer systems commonly found in classroom use
- information technology across the curriculum
- effective uses of book and object resources

Working with other adults in the classroom. KEY ISSUE: Relating to adults in school.

Other responsibilities

YOU WILL NEED TO LEARN ABOUT

- the significance of staff team membership, collaborative planning and collegiality
- the function of support staff and their responsibilities
- the importance of collaborative planning
- utilising colleagues' expertise in your teaching

Working with other adults outside the classroom KEY ISSUE: Teamwork

YOU WILL NEED TO LEARN ABOUT

- staff structures
- curriculum leadership and management
- professional relationships
- mutual support and encouragement

YOU WILL NEED TO LEARN ABOUT

- safety first
- common causes of injury or distress
- the importance of setting a good example to your pupils.

Health and safety KEY ISSUE: Security

Remember that you are not expected to achieve all the above criteria by your first week in school! The statements provide a set of descriptions about key aspects of teaching which can be used as a framework to monitor your progress, establish your priorities and give your teaching experience a sense of direction and purpose. You do not have to achieve all of these competences immediately, but by the end of your training course. In reality, although you cannot expect to be an expert in everything, you should aim to achieve as much as you can through your college work and teaching opportunities. If you can demonstrate through your practical teaching that you are progressing well in key areas (notably the core subjects and your subject specialism), you will have success as a teacher within your grasp.

It is also important to remember that teachers do not only teach children; they also have to relate to other adults, prepare documentation, supervise activities, and take the lead in planing educational visits, assemblies and whole school celebrations. Your own determination, consideration for others, friendly manner and sense of responsibility will help you to achieve far more than you imagined possible.

AT THE END OF A SCHOOL EXPERIENCE

Your time in school may have been agony or ecstasy, or perhaps a little of both. You may have exceeded or fallen below your expectations. The children may have been a delight or the cause of desperation. Whatever your experience, your final day in school always brings a mixture of emotions.

One emotion will be *relief* that the pressure is lifting and you can return to normal, with no more lesson preparation, evaluations, negotiating with supervisors, trying to convince everyone that you really knew what you were doing. No more fretting over being unable to cope; no more worrying that the other students in the school were doing better than you; no more dread of humiliation; no more fear of failure.

A second emotion will be one of *regret* over leaving the school, losing your influence in the children's education, walking away from a situation that has been an intimate part of your life for the past few weeks or months. As the last afternoon approaches, you may be quite overcome with anguish; children sometimes cry when they hear that you are leaving and they bring small gifts of hastily made cards and other tokens of affection. When the class teacher prepares to take over from you in the areas of teaching for which you were responsible, it comes as a shock to realise that you are expendable, and that in a short time the children will no longer speak your name, ask your advice, rely upon your judgement or respond to your directions. You will become aware that the intimacy of the relationships were transitory for nearly all the children, and that you were only a small spark in the furnace of their education and development.

Nevertheless, it is important to remind yourself that you *have* made a difference and that there are many other children waiting for you to arrive through the classroom door, enquire of you whether you are a real teacher, test your mettle, and engage with you in learning. Next time you will be a little wiser and more certain of your ability to cope and prosper. One thing is certain, if you persevere and work hard during your school experiences, the day will come when you step across the classroom threshold and hear yourself saying to the children:

'Good morning, everyone; I'm your new class teacher'

Appendix

General

Are you familiar with

- the school's dress code?
- the location and availability of resources?
- the names of teaching and non-teaching staff?
- the times that ancillary staff are in school, and the extent of their duties?
- the school's policy for relating to parents?
- extra-curricular activities?
- the type of personal possessions that children may bring to school?

Procedures

Have you made a note of

- timetabling of breaks, hall times, and so on?
- registration procedures?
- lunchtime procedures?
- systems for borrowing and changing books, taking books home, and so on?
- fire drill and safety in school?
- the school's behaviour policy?

Organisation

Do you know about the way learning is organised

- in the main classroom teaching area?
- in additional work areas?
- through the use of different resources and equipment?
- through use of display space and displaying children's work?
- with respect to the extent of children's movement, independence and choice?

Curriculum

Are you familiar with

- the school's medium-term plans?
- the work children have recently covered?
- schemes of work (or similar)?
- records of achievement or baseline assessments?
- the teacher's approach to the teaching of reading?
- the teacher's approach to the teaching of number?
- the use of TV broadcasts?

Teaching approaches

Do you have a grasp of the way in which the class teacher

- uses group and whole class methods?
- uses collaborative groupwork for problem solving and investigation?
- organises the teaching of children with special needs?
- uses texts, worksheets, games, and other teaching aids?
- monitors children's progress and offers feedback?
- assesses and records children's progress?

Your responsibilities

Have you

- reviewed your progress on previous school experiences?
- reflected on priorities for the practice?
- agreed precise details of your commitments with the class teacher?
- gained a preliminary idea of the range and extent of your teaching commitment and other responsibilities across your school experience?

Professional behaviour

Have you given sufficient thought to

- the time it takes to travel to the school?
- the occasions you will stay behind after school?
- the strengths that you bring to the school?
- the impression that you are creating with staff, parents and children?

Bibliography

Alexander, R.J., Rose, A.J. and Woodhead, C. (1992) *Curriculum Organisation and Classroom Practice in Primary Schools: A Discussion Paper*. London: DfE.

Bowley, R.L. (1961) *Teaching Without Tears*. London: Centaur Press.

Clark, M.M. (1994) *Young Literacy Learners*. Leamington Spa: Scholastic Publications.

Cox, T. and Sanders, S. (1994) *The Impact of the National Curriculum On Five Year Olds*. London: Falmer Press.

Department for Education (1992) *Initial Teacher Training: Secondary Phase*. Circular 9/92. London: DfE.

Department for Education (1993) *The Initial Training of Primary School Teachers: New Criteria for Courses* (Circular 14/93). London: DfE.

Department for Education (1995) *The National Curriculum*. London: HMSO. (containing details of each subject area)

Dunne, R. and Wragg, E.C. (1994) *Effective Teaching*. London: Routledge.

Fisher, R. (1995) *Teaching Children To Learn*. Cheltenham: Stanley Thornes.

Furlong, J. and Maynard, T. (1995) *Mentoring Student Teachers*. London: Routledge.

Harrop, A. and Holmes, T. (1993) 'Teachers' perceptions of their pupils' views on rewards and punishments', in *Pastoral Care in Education*, vol. 11, No. 1, pages 30–5.

Hayes, D. (1996) *Foundations of Primary Teaching*. London: David Fulton.

Hewett, I.V. (1984) *Number Games for Younger Children*. Nantwich: Shiva Publishing.

Lawrence, D. (1996) *Enhancing Self Esteem in the Classroom*. London: Paul Chapman Publishing.

Lewis, M. and Wray, D. (1995) *Developing Children's Non-Fiction Writing*. Leamington Spa: Scholastic Publications.

Mills, J. and Mills, R.W. (1995) *Primary School People*. London: Routledge.

Moyles, J. (1992) *Organising for Learning in the Primary Classroom*. Buckingham: Open University Press.

National Curriculum Council (1993) *The National Curriculum at Key Stages 1 and 2*. London: NCC.

Nias, D.J. (1989) *Primary Teachers Talking*. London: Routledge.

Office for Standards in Education (1993) *Curriculum Organisation and Classroom Practice in Primary Schools: A Follow Up Report*. London: OFSTED.

Proctor, A., Entwistle, M., Judge, B. and McKenzie-Murdoch, S. (1995) *Learning to Teach in the Primary Classroom*. London: Routledge.

Pye, J. (1988) *Invisible Children*. Oxford: Oxford University Press.

Robertson, J. (1996) *Effective Classroom Control* (third edition). London: Hodder and Stoughton.

School Curriculum and Assessment Authority (1995) *Exemplification of Standards in English, Mathematics and Science*. London: SCAA Publications.

Teacher Training Agency (1997) Consultation On the Training Curriculum and Standards for New Teachers. London: TTA.

Topping, K. (1995) *Paired Reading, Spelling and Writing*. London: Cassell Education.

Index